*"Deeply touching, uplifting, and challenging . . . <u>Seasons of the Spirit</u> was exactly what I needed and at just the right time. The last two days were spent 'close to the vines' where once again I felt the goosebumps of your stirring message."*

Helen McEnerney
Vice President and General Manager
Del Webb California Corp.

*"<u>Seasons of the Spirit</u> is a winner!"*

Alvin Dark
Member of the Baseball Hall of Fame

Preparing for the Best Half
of Life's Journey

Seasons
of
the

Spirit

WARD TANNEBERG AND STEPHEN TAYLOR

LION
PUBLISHING

Lion Publishing
A Division of Cook Communications,
4050 Lee Vance View,
Colorado Springs, CO 80918

Editor: Barb Williams
Design: Bill Gray
Images: Image Bank

"Grow old along with me!

The best is yet to be,

the last of life, for which the first was made;

Our times are in His hand

Who saith, 'A whole I planned,

Youth shows but half;

trust God: see all, nor be afraid!'"

—Robert Browning in "Rabbi ben Ezra"


"Baby boomers [are] the

first generation in history

to enter midlife with the prospect of

four more decades of life-expectancy ...

The question is: what will we

make of it?"

—Dr. Jack Rowe,
MacArthur Fellow
President, Mt. Sinai Medical Center,
New York City

# Dedication

In memory of Ras and Luella Janneberg

who taught me that

every person can and should

make a difference.

—Ward


and to

J. C. and Theresa Taylor

who taught me to

love stories,

and who read me

the greatest story at an early age.

—Steve

# Foreword

I've spent the last the twenty-five years of my life seeking to alert America to the changing demographic landscape—the "age wave"—and the need to modify our image of aging. Thankfully, as the last years of the century wind down, it appears that finally we have begun to embrace a more positive, active, and promising picture of what a new generation of middle-aged and older adults in America can be and do.

But with all the emerging books, newspaper articles, and television programs on diet, exercise, and retirement living, one facet of the aging experience has remained largely unexplored: the metaphysical, the spiritual. It is an aspect of my own personal aging about which I have only recently begun to reflect and ponder. It was for that reason I was pleased to pick up and read this volume. Pleased both for what the book is and for what it is not.

Make no mistake: if you think you are holding in your hands another fluffy, mystical journey to nowhere, be prepared to be surprised. *Seasons of the Spirit* is an optimistic, practical, readable, and doable guide to nurturing the spiritual facet at the center of our lives for the ride through the second half of the lifespan.

The human spirit has been probed and pricked, contemplated and investigated by every modern generation. There is a reason for that. As authors Tanneberg and Taylor point out, "The human spirit is the part of us that God touches." In that respect, *Seasons of the Spirit* joins a long line of efforts to deal with this truth.

In this enjoyable volume, however, the authors have skillfully tied the search for answers to "the big questions"—the hunger of the human spirit—to the midlife experience common to most baby boomers. The search Tanneberg and Taylor take us on is not a wilderness journey through a desert of dry philosophical concepts and theological terms. To the contrary: concise, imaginative writing and the ancient tools of storytelling and allegory make paragraphs flow and pages turn easily with an engaging freshness.

We are reminded of the many signposts along the life-path, familiar to us all, marking our passages and progress through time. They welcome us to our twenties. Graduations. Weddings. Births. We whirl past them during our thirties. Another birth perhaps. A promotion. Our first house. We wander by them, thoughtfully, through our forties. College for the kids. A new family car. Another promotion. A move to a new city.

And along the way are the unexpected twists and turns. The unhappy events we didn't plan on. Divorce. Illness. Job loss. Financial reversals. Deaths. As we mature, we experience them with our eyes wide open.

As we pass each of these bridges, we find ourselves hopeful, wary, and asking new questions. Who am I really at this time in my life? Where am I headed? Can I control what happens from here on? What about the looming shadows of my failures and past disappointments? Will my successes continue? What does the future hold—or not hold—for me?

*Seasons of the Spirit* melds today, yesterday, and tomorrow into a simple guidebook for finding and crossing over the living bridges of our lives, from one decade to another, from one lifestage event to the next. The story lets us follow a midlife couple named Adam and Eva in their quest for personal and spiritual meaning. And as we do, the authors provide an extremely creative way for the quest to become our own. We join Adam and Eva in learning to "listen with our eyes and see with our hearts," and in the process learn something about our own quest for happiness, completeness, and closure in the years after our youth.

Tanneberg and Taylor guide us through the seasons of the human spirit in a delightful and refreshing way. Like good friends, they pause with us now and then to help us reflect on our own view of the things we are seeing along the way. Less a map, more a travelogue, *Seasons* helps us to reexamine and redefine our life at the midpoint and to gain control through elevated awareness. Although the authors write unapologetically from within a Christian worldview, they are gentle in inviting all of us to test the relevance of ancient truths to our current and personal concerns.

America's baby boomers are on the cusp of realizing the human dream—to live longer than any generation in history. With the gift of time comes a desire and responsibility to use it wisely. As I have traveled the country over the past twenty-five years, I have asked literally millions of people to consider: "What will you make of the rest of your life?" Having succeeded at adding those years to our lives, we must now find our way in adding life to our years.

*Seasons of the Spirit* will help you do just that—and more. It will make you think. It will touch your feelings. It will stir your faith. It did mine.

Ken Dychtwald, Ph.D.
President and CEO, Age Wave, Inc.

# Introduction

On January 1, 1996, the first 7,745 of 76 million baby boomers celebrated their fiftieth birthday. By the end of that year, 3.4 million had passed the fifty-year milestone. For fifteen years boomers will continue "crossing over the bar," sailing toward retirement age. As early as 2005, boomers will become a majority of those aged fifty to seventy-four.

Leaving aside their foreseeable impact on the midlife marketplace, the years surrounding fifty and beyond are certain to be a time of frustration and radical change in life status that will disturb and unsettle millions of boomers.

When a sample of Americans was asked if they had experienced any trauma during the past twelve months, the highest percentage reported was among those in their late forties [49 percent] and early fifties [53 percent]. These crises of midlife invariably centered in matters of family, jobs, and personal health.

The death of a parent, for example, is one of the most traumatic events people go through in their late forties or early fifties. The percentage of people with mothers still living falls from 74 percent among forty-to-forty-four-year-olds to just 34 percent among fifty-five-to-fifty-nine-year-olds. With living fathers the drop is even faster, from 57 percent among forty-to-forty-four-year-olds to 31 percent among forty-five-to-forty-nine-year-olds.[1]

Midlife introduces a spate of new issues and opportu-

---

[1] 1994 Gen. Social Survey by Nat'l Opinion Research Center, U. of Chicago. Reported by Russell, Cheryl, *The Baby Boom Turns 50*, Dec. 1995. American Demographics, Inc.

nities when children leave the nest, the daily tedium takes its toll, and the first twinges of chronic illness or pain are felt on a regular basis. Boomers over fifty will face everything from corporate downsizing to toxic waste clean up. From rising divorce rates to mounting health care costs. With a feeling that so much that matters is beyond their control, as in times of war or other great crises, many will shop for quick fixes and new-age cures, while others turn within to search for core values and balance points to give life meaning and perspective.

*Seasons of the Spirit* is presented as an easily read story that highlights what we have learned from our studies and the experience gained through our years of working with many people in the enrichment of their personal lives.

By "enrichment" we mean how people increase the desirable quality and ingredients of their lives, feel good about themselves, the world around them, and the people they see and interact with every day.

This allegory is a simple compilation of what others have taught us and what we have learned in the living of life ourselves, having both earned our own set of "mid-life credentials." It focuses on a universal question asked at various ages and stages in life, and especially as we approach that mysterious fifty-year mid-life marker. We're curious. Even a little concerned. So much so that, when we think no one else is watching, we stand on our tiptoes, trying to see beyond to what is ahead. It is the question that, in many ways, controls and defines who we are and how we view ourselves:

*"What am I going to do with the rest of my life?"*

*Seasons of the Spirit* presents seven specific principles that address this question in an introspective and insightful attempt to help our readers find the way to their own individual answers.

The practical knowledge gained from this book will be useful for readers and those around them, in achieving happier, more fulfilling and satisfying lives.

Ward Tanneberg, Ph.D.
Stephen Taylor, Ph.D.

# Seasons of the Spirit

*E*ndings invariably contain the seeds of new beginnings.

It's true.

Life's rhythms are simple, yet profound. First an ending, followed by inevitable chaos, and finally, a new beginning.

"Unless a kernel of wheat falls to the ground and dies, it remains only a single seed," Jesus Christ once said. "But if it dies, it produces many seeds." [2]

Endings.

Chaos.

New beginnings.

On occasion, they confront us in the guise of our own Choices. While at other times they arrive on the wings of Surprise. One thing is sure, though. Only on television do life's episodes work themselves out in sixty minutes and still leave ample time for commercials and station breaks. These rhythmic patterns regularly flow through the seasons of the human spirit, requiring time to complete their work within us.

Seasons of the spirit come and go, surge and wane. They aren't governed by tides or controlled by temperatures

---

[2] The Bible. John 12:24.

or anticipated by calendars. They are influenced by events in our lives, swayed by our emotions, and shaped by our attitudes. The seasonal outlook for weather can only be predicted, then endured or enjoyed. Seasons of the spirit, however, give us potential for perspective, the promise of opportunity, and a possibility for growth and fulfillment.

Since the dawn of Creation, man has searched for the meaning and purpose of life. Scientists examine the minutia of protoplasm and the mystery of planets. Philosophers ponder the imponderable. Theologians muse over the inner life and the other life. And ordinary people are left to wander and wonder, and to feel that even if it were explained they would not understand or ever be able to maximize life's potential for themselves. For the truly disillusioned, life's fulfillment is reduced to manipulated responses prompted by television commercials and newspaper ads.

Still, we keep exploring. We visit places of worship, attend lectures, participate in seminars, listen to audio tapes, "surf the Net," and even read books. Yet so much of what we uncover appears not to be connected with the life we live. It all seems so ethereal ... abstract ... metaphysical. Where did we miss it? If only there were a simple way, a way that we could understand. A way to plow through myriad tomes and textbooks, connect the physical and spiritual, and touch the Creator of all things.

Here's how it was done in ages past.

Employing the universal power of Story, a single family was chosen for purposes of illustration. History came later, providing an essential rootedness in the ever-expanding garden of man. The warnings of seers and prophets called people to accountable living. Don't make it harder than it already is, they cautioned. Wise words, indeed.

At last, we are told, someOne stepped into our history. SomeOne unique and different from others. An extraordinary man, who lived in otherwise ordinary places, among ordinary people, circumstances, and times. His thoughts were viewed as ingenious, even revolutionary, yet his ways remained wrapped in commonality. By word and example, he taught those who would listen how it should be. "Remain in me," he said, "and I will remain in you. No branch can bear fruit by itself; it must remain in the vine." [3]

Doesn't it cause you to wonder? Why would someOne speak in this fashion? How did so grand a story as was begun in the Garden of Creation shrink to such a simple analogy drawn from a local vineyard?

It's easy to grasp when you understand the power of Story.

Story has been the strong friend of the people through the ages, enlightening, lifting us higher on its shoulders, so that we might see the unseeable and know the unknowable through ancient Greek mythologists like Euripides; the prince of English literature, William Shakespeare; a turn-of-the-century Tolstoy, and modern mega-sellers like Mary Higgins Clark and John Grisham. Yet each of these pay respectful tribute to the Greatest Story Teller of all—Jesus Christ.

He left not a single page written by his own hand, yet through parables, allegories, and illustrations of all kinds, he has given insight to puzzled minds and peace to countless troubled hearts. One would expect such a man to select

---

[3] The Bible. John 15:4.

carefully, from the innumerable choices at his disposal, the best insights to help us find the things that make life work. And he does not disappoint us. Out of all things living, he chooses the common vineyard to make his point.

He knew that the insights inherent in the vine and branch would ever be accessible to all. Good for any age. Especially so when the decades are stacked like cordwood behind us and the first twinges of age-pain take up residence in our joints. Especially so when, deep in our hearts, we long to keep time with the music of the universe, to dance in celebration of immortality, and to follow the familiar guiding hands of the Director as we experience the symphony of life's seasons.

But how is this possible? How can we rise from the obscurity of an inferior condition to touch something and someOne so much higher and greater than ourselves? The answer is not to be found in what the empowerment seminars and corporate gurus have sought to teach us. Does it mean that they've been wrong? Not altogether. It's just that they can take us only part way.

If the total of one's life were centered in position and power and possessions we would need go no further. We can be taught how to get there [position], stay there [power], and buy there [possessions]. We can experience the fruits of independence and self-indulgence [pleasure]. But still, we are left with the question that haunts us, even if it remains unuttered. Is this all there is to life?

Our own generation embraced moral law as relative, judged philosophy paradoxical, and declared religion to be totally subjective. We've been pillaged by the mind manipulators who broke down the doors of reason and authority, raped and sacked and robbed our past recollections, and left us with few, if any, absolutes. The Western intellect was loosed from its moorings and set adrift in a trackless sea of speculation. Formulas abounded from Wall Street to Main Street for making a million, but not for molding a life.

It was a breathless first-half, full of schools, jobs, family—and lots and lots of dreams. Until we bounced across one of life's speedbumps! We knew all along it was out there ahead of us, and yet did not see it. We were going much too fast for that. It jolts us. Our head hits the underside of the rooftop. Our foot feels for the brake. Tires squeal. We don't exactly hurt ourselves, but we do manage to feel a little foolish.

A sign says, "Slow Down."

*Slow down?*

Just when we've reached maximum warp speed, someOne wants us to slow down? We look around, grumble a bit, then grudgingly give ourselves permission. Not much, you understand, just a little slower. For now. At least while someOne is watching.

Then comes the letter. Should we laugh or cry? Instead of a ticket for speeding through life, our invitation to AARP shows up in the mail. We are welcomed into the Fellowship of the Fifty-Plus, somewhat dazed, yet relieved that we've arrived safely, and mystified as to where the years that brought us here have gone.

For some of us, at this stage of life, the siren song of career has become hollow and even discordant. Our capacity for success appears to have been measured for us by others, often without the benefit of seeking our opinion or asking about our dreams.

So have the times of trauma that often accompany one's late forties and fifties. The failing health or death of a parent confronts us with our own mortality. The values and behaviors of the "younger generation" [so recently us!] seem foreign and uncivilized. Even our own children disappoint, and that threatens us. The excitement with which we used to wake up each morning is on the wane.

Achievers compensate by quietly declaring this to be the time for making and spending the most money, for reveling in the power posts of government and business, for enjoying the perks of country clubs and corporate jets, immersing themselves in the accolades of success as measured by an acquisitive society.

Others commiserate as days of rapid promotion and pay increases give way to predictability and pallidness. Fifteen or twenty more years of work before arriving at an uncertain retirement seems more like a prison sentence than a sparkling promise.

Still, one way or another—walking, crawling, or by doing nothing more than simply "making it," we finally arrive at the ending of the first half-century of self-life. We have a past, albeit a mixed bag. Many rejoicings, some regrets. But do we have a future? Will it be more of the same? Will our life after fifty be frustrating and failing? Or will it be fun ... fulfilling ... and fruitful?

The ancient writers record the Great Story Teller's thoughts on this question. Musings that are filled with branches and vines, grapes and bonfires. At first, we're tempted to toss them aside and check out today's stock prices and tomorrow's headlines. But wait. Slow down. It's a great story, an allegory, with insights just waiting to be plucked.

The theme of this book is chosen with good reason, for when we discover the secrets of the vineyard we can better understand and move within the seasons of the human spirit. We find our way across the changing landscape of our lives, by learning to respond rather than reject, to love rather than hate, to fill up rather than be fed up. And in the process, we discover answers to questions of the shape of life to come after fifty!

How can it happen for you?

Come with us to a special place. One filled with timeless truth. You should be forewarned that the best way is to go slowly, meditatively. Take your time. Pause once in a while. Sip each reminder and every refreshing thought as you would the finest of wines. Carefully now, peel away the obvious and discover hidden layers of meaning that point you toward happiness and fulfillment.

Vineyard, courtyard, backyard—it really doesn't matter. A weekend retreat. A walk in the woods. An evening at home alone. Lunch break at the office. Flying across the country. With the power of Story, you can create an oasis for the human spirit almost anywhere—if you will "listen with your eyes and see with your heart."

Come on. Let's do it!

**Acquiescence.** To be quiet and accepting; to surrender passively; to agree with something after careful consideration.

**Patience.** To bear pains or trials calmly, without complaint; to remain steadfast despite opposition, difficulty, or adversity.

**Emergence.** To become manifest; visible; to rise from an obscure or inferior condition.

**Interior Insight #1**

Acquiescence + Patience = Emergence.

Once there was an old man who had spent his entire life caring for a vineyard inherited from his father. As he lay dying, the old man called for his only son and daughter-in-law, who lived in The City, and informed them that all the vines were now theirs.

———

"Stay close to the vineyard, my children," he whispered, as a faint, but loving smile prompted more wrinkles in his weathered face. "Learn to listen with your eyes and see with your hearts. If you do, the vines will share with you the secret of happiness."

From the window, his son and daughter-in-law looked out on row after row of frail, grotesque vines that seemed as emaciated as the old man's body. The harvest was past. Winter hovered a short distance away, behind the hills, tempered by autumn's persistence. In the distance, cars hurried steadily in both directions and flashes of sunlight reflected on the metallic skin of an airplane high above the landscape.

The son shook his head sadly and glanced at his wife. He loved his father, but what could he mean? He's obviously not himself. He appears to be stuck in another time and place. In a world that is dying, not the real world. The real world was stirring, moving, pulsating all around them. Out there. Beyond the naked branches that stretched in front of them like the wasted arms of vine-martyrs.

"Promise that you will stay close to the vineyard, my children," the old man urged once again.

"I promise," said the son, not wanting to upset his dying father.

"And I as well," answered the son's wife, wiping his furrowed brow with a damp cloth.

"The secret of happiness is in the vineyard," he croaked again, pointing his shaky hand toward the window. "Tell it to your children. Be certain that Seth and Carrie learn the secret."

"How can I be certain when I don't know what it is myself?" asked the son.

"You will," sighed the old man, reaching out his open palm to touch first his son, then his daughter-in-law, as though somehow anointing them for the task. "You will.

And remember, when the time comes, each of your children must learn the secret for themselves to ensure their own happiness."

"All right, Father," replied the son, gathering the thin callused hand in his. "I'll try."

"And I will try as well," affirmed the daughter-in-law again.

That night the old man died.

They dressed him in his Sunday clothes along with one of the few ties found in his closet. "Always like lookin' my best," he would say, "when goin' to a formal meetin' with the Lord." Mourners smiled and brushed at their eyes as they passed by, seeing the old floppy work hat perched on his chest, a familiar reminder of the many times he had waved a greeting from the vineyard, inevitably concluded by his bony fingers touching its well-worn brim in friendly salute.

He was laid to rest beneath the gnarled branches of an oak tree that sheltered a gentle slope near the eastern edge of the vineyard, not far from a small spring of clear running water. It seemed fitting. After the old man's neighbors had wished the family well and said their good-byes, the grandchildren drove into town, while the son and his wife stayed behind to wander across the vineyard. They held hands as they walked, each consoling the other, not so much with words, but simply by being together in this place.

They laughed about it later, remarking how foolish they felt, both admitting to actually having tried to listen ... and look ... for something while walking among the vines.

The wife confessed disappointment after returning to the house. The old man's son nodded. He felt it too.

But there had been nothing. Nothing but emptiness.

Even the vines seemed to droop in the knowledge that their owner was gone.

The next day was the same.

And the next.

*O*n the fourth day, the son got up early to walk among the vine rows. The air was crisp and the morning sky had dressed in a uniform of blue-gray to greet the rising sun. What few leaves remained, shivering on the vines, were hard and brittle and broke off easily in his hand. For some reason, he felt even sadder than on previous days.

Then he saw him.

A man in scruffy work clothes, walking in his direction.

At first he thought to turn away for he wasn't in the mood to meet anyone. Being alone was what he really wanted. He glanced about, but there was no opening available to move to the next row. He was trapped. The man kept coming.

"You look like him, Adam," the dark-skinned stranger said matter-of-factly, as they approached one another. "You are your father's son all right. I knew it the minute I saw you at the grave."

"I am," Adam replied. "But I'm sorry, I don't remember you."

"I know. I didn't want to bother you the other day. There were so many people. My name is Juan. I've worked many years for your father. You were away and he needed someone to help with the vines."

"Of course. Dad has spoken of you often. I've been gone too many years. I was young when I went away to school and I never came back. Not to live or work, that is. Only for an occasional visit." Adam paused to await a response. None came, so he continued his confession. "I guess I really am a 'City person' now. I don't know much about the vines at all."

For some reason, Adam felt a sudden eagerness to talk to this man with the soft, lyrical voice, whose "i's" often sounded like "e's" and whose "r's" rolled off his tongue like birdsong. A pleasant Hispanic man who had worked beside his father for so many years. He couldn't help but stare. It was like seeing a missing part of his own life. "Juan, we don't really know each other, but could I ask you something personal?"

"I know you quite well actually," Juan responded.

Adam looked at him in surprise.

"Your father spoke of you often. He told me all about you and your family, where you live and work. And about his grandchildren, Seth and Carrie. He was very proud of you, Adam."

"You have me at a disadvantage. I always thought that he was a little disappointed in me," Adam blurted out, at the same time thinking how unlike him it was to share such a private feeling with a total stranger. *But he isn't a stranger, is he? This man worked with my father.*

"Why did you think that?" Juan asked curiously.

"Because I went away. I guess the truth is I've always felt a little guilty that I didn't stay here to work the vineyard with Dad." Adam motioned at the vines with a sweep of his hand. "This was his life."

"Every man must live his own life," Juan responded gently. "Your father knew that. He loved you enough to let you go. He knew your place was 'out there,' not here."

Adam remained silent, reining in emotions that unexpectedly welled up from within. At last he cleared his throat and spoke again.

"Dad said something strange to Eva ... that's my wife ... but then you probably know about her too, don't you?"

Juan nodded, his smile patient and forbearing. Waiting.

"Well, Dad said something very strange to Eva and me the day he died," Adam began again. "We've been trying to figure it out ever since. He was so emphatic. He made us promise to stay close to the vineyard. I thought at the time that he might be worried we would sell it or something. Then he said 'Listen with your eyes and see with your heart.' Doesn't that seem odd? And if we did, he said, 'The vine will share with you the secret of happiness.' Those were his exact words. Oh, and he also insisted that we pass on the secret to our children. I said that would be difficult, in that I didn't know what he was talking about."

"And what was his response?"

"'You will.' That was all he said. Just, 'you will.' I'm not sure he was all there mentally when he said it, and I've still no clue as to what he might have meant. I feel a little foolish, you know? Still, here I am. I've been out here in the vineyard every day since we buried him under that tree over there."

"And?"

"And nothing. I'm at a complete loss as to what to make of it."

Juan smiled, looking down as he kicked at the dirt with the toe of his boot. "Your father was a very wise man."

"I know. But he was old too and I think he might have been losing touch with reality at the end."

"No," Juan said reassuringly, "he was more in touch with life than most folk."

"Then what was he talking about? He always carried such a feeling of passion and romance surrounding this whole viticulture thing. Sometimes it was all he could talk about. Don't you think he might possibly have been drifting between that romance and reality?"

"He told you to 'listen with your eyes?' 'to see with your heart?'"

"Yes."

"Then I can assure you he was not 'drifting.' That is what you must do."

"But how? I don't have a clue as to what that means, let alone how to do it."

Juan hesitated. "Do you really want to know?" he asked finally.

"Of course."

"It will take some time."

"Actually, that's one thing I have plenty of at the moment. My job in The City ended two weeks ago. The Company is downsizing. They call it early retirement, but it feels like I've been fired. Let go. Persona non grata."

"I'm sorry."

"Me too. I poured my life into The Company for the last ten years. I thought I'd be there until I retired."

"Did your father know?"

Adam shook his head. "There was no point in worrying him. It's not fair, though, is it? They expect you to work hard, be loyal, make sacrifices, the whole bit. And this is what you get in return. Ten years, Juan. I get angry just thinking about it."

"Perhaps you're ready then."

"Ready for what?"

"To see ... and to hear."

Adam looked at Juan for a long moment. "You honestly think there's something real in what he was saying?"

"I know there is. But to understand it for yourself, you must approach the promise with a sincere desire to learn. It will take time," he emphasized once again.

"Yeah, you said that. How much time?"

Juan paused, gazing steadily into Adam's eyes.

"One year, at least."

"Are you kidding?" exclaimed Adam. "I can't sit around here for a whole year waiting for a stupid vineyard to say something, for pete's sake! Besides, vines don't talk. It's ludicrous! I'm staying for a few weeks to wrap things up, of course, but by then, I should be getting some job interviews. The first copies of my resumé went into the mail yesterday."

Juan gazed steadily at the ground and continued rearranging the soil with the toe of his boot. "Then you will miss it," he said finally, a touch of sadness in his eyes as he looked up.

"What do you mean?"

"You'll miss what your father promised."

"You mean this 'seeing and hearing' business?"

"No. That's only the process."

"Then what?"

"Happiness."

"What?"

"He promised you the secret of happiness, didn't he?"

"Yes," Adam responded slowly, "as a matter of fact, he did."

"Then I'm sorry. I know you are busy." The dark-skinned man started to walk away.

"Wait," Adam called after him.

Juan hesitated and then turned back. He said nothing.

"I don't even know why I'm talking about this. It's all too absurd. But ... well, I am tired. I haven't taken a real vacation in years. Perhaps I could stay for ... say, three months ... " Adam conceded reluctantly.

Juan waited.

"Okay. I need some time off and they did give me a pretty good severance package," he added grudgingly. "Maybe six, tops."

The man in boots, grubby pants, and worn jacket shrugged.

"Nine?" Adam grimaced as the word shaped on his lips.

The beginnings of a slight smile formed on Juan's face, but still, he said nothing.

"What's the big deal about an entire year?" Adam cried out, throwing his hands up in exasperation.

"That's how long it was before I learned the secret."

"You?" Adam's voice softened with surprise. "You

know the secret? Did my father ... " His words trailed off.

"Yes, he said these same things when I came to work here. At first, I wondered like you. I didn't understand what he meant either. But he was a special man, your father. And this is a special place."

"But ... a year ... "

Juan shrugged again.

"Perhaps you will discover it more quickly. After all, you are a college graduate and your father has often said that you're very smart." His demeanor was not at all rude as he spoke, but serious and respectful. "I'm sorry to say, however, your intelligence and training may make it even harder. For you to learn the secret and apply it to your own life ... I think it will take one year, at least."

"But why so long?" asked Adam in exasperation.

"It takes time to experience the seasons," Juan replied simply.

"The seasons? You mean the growing cycle of the grapes?"

Juan shook his head.

"This is not about the seasons of the grapes," he answered.

"No?"

"No."

"Then what?"

"It's about the seasons of the spirit."

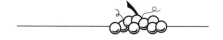

*Start Thinking About Your Own*

*"Spiritual Dimension"*

Using percentages that total 100%, estimate how much time in your daily life the following three dimensions presently occupy:

The Physical Dimension —health, body, hygiene _____%

The Mental Dimension —ideas, thoughts, emotions _____%

The Spiritual Dimension—purpose, meaning, God _____%

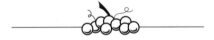

*Periods*
*of dormancy*
*are a normal*
*part of life,*
*essential to*
*restoration.*
*They constitute*
*the Winter*
*Season.*

*B*y the time Adam walked through the front door, Eva was in the kitchen preparing breakfast. Seth, their oldest, a senior at City College, was driving back to the campus this morning. Carrie, in her first collegiate year, was going with him. Both still lived at home with their parents, though Seth was talking about moving out after graduation.

Adam felt a sudden flush of pride as they sat down together at the table. Eva looked so beautiful, hair tied back, no make-up, a simple blouse and jeans. The children were good kids too. He worried that Carrie was too much of a free spirit, but her mother assured him that she would settle down in time. After all, she was just eighteen. When breakfast was over, they kissed and hugged. The children promised to call when they got home that night. And then they were gone.

Adam and Eva pulled on sweaters, took their cups onto the veranda, and stood looking out over the vineyard while Adam told her about meeting Juan and his insistence that they needed to stay a year to fulfill their promise to his father.

"What did you say to him?" Eva asked cautiously, creases of concern marking her brow as she looked at her husband.

"I told him we would talk about it ... and let him know tomorrow."

"Why does he have to know? What business is it of his what we do anyway?"

"He said he would help us. Apparently he knows something about this big secret. The one Dad was talking about. At least that's what he claims. Anyway, who can tell? He said that if we stayed, he would help us ... you know ... with the vine stuff and all." Adam looked quizzically at his bride of twenty-four years, a sheepish grin on his face. "And when I say that out loud, it sounds totally stupid, doesn't it?"

"Completely."

A long silence settled between them. Finally, Eva took his hand.

"You want to stay, don't you?"

"I don't know. I'm confused. It was kind of funny, standing out there though, talking to that guy. I started to feel like there's something here that I don't understand. In fact, the whole time since Dad died, it's as though a part of me is trying to break out that I didn't know existed before. I can't explain it, but talking to this Juan character was almost like talking with Dad. Maybe it's crazy, but ... I've been thinking that he probably knows Dad better and has spent more time with him than I have."

Eva watched him as he talked.

"So you want to stay?" she repeated.

Adam was quiet. Then slowly he nodded his head. "For a little while, maybe."

"Until your eyes listen?" she asked with a mischievous smile.

He slipped his arm around her waist.

"And until your heart sees," he replied with his own half grin.

The next day, Adam and Eva walked into the vineyard together. This was the time of year he liked the least under normal circumstances. Today was no different. Everything was so dry and dead and out of order. The field had a beaten down, impotent look. Row after row of vines stretched lifelessly along stakes and wires, desolate and malformed.

"They're not dead. They're exhausted."

Both started at the sound of the voice behind them. They had not heard Juan approaching.

"Why did you say the vines are exhausted?" asked Eva after they had greeted one another.

"Because it's true. It's why they look so forlorn. For months they've poured themselves into their work, twenty-four hours a day, seven days a week, without a break."

"You talk about them as though they were people," said Adam.

"I think about them in that way," answered Juan. "Their reason for being, their calling, so to speak, is to produce grapes. Unlike we humans, the vines are clear on that matter and center all their energies on fulfilling their purpose in life. To be successful each vine has to set down deep roots, develop to maturity, and nurture a positive relationship with the other vines, as well as the grower and the Creator. Each one, and every vineyard too, has its own personality."

"I'm not sure I follow you."

"See these vines around us? They produce the Chardonnay grape. They're perfect for this locale. The soil, the temperature, everything here is right for these vines to succeed. Further up the valley a few miles, the Cabernet Sauvignon, and the Zinfandel are grown. And those are only three of many kinds of grapes grown around the world, each chosen for its capacity to live and produce in a given region. Look here, for example. See the fertile clay? But off to the north the soil consists of gravel loams with better drainage and lower fertility."

"Environment is crucial then?"

"Of course. There must be the right amounts of sun, water, shade, soil, fertilizer. And constant attention from the grower. In fact, it's said that growing grapes is the most labor-intensive of all agricultural pursuits."

"But now things look so ... barren and bleak," Eva commented, arms folded as she surveyed the vineyard.

"The vines are as they should be."

"What do you mean?"

"They're resting. Taking time to prepare themselves for another harvest. There will be work enough to do later, producing buds and blossoms and fruit. Dormancy is essential to the well-being of the vine. To us it appears that nothing is happening here. But the vines know better. Even now, they're carefully restoring their depleted inner resources. Resources that will carry them all the way through *véraison*."

"Véraison?"

"The beginning of the final growth period for the grape. You see, the grape berry goes through three growth stages. Your father used to say that they're like the three stages of life. During Stage One, hormones are running around, making possible the growth and retention of the berry on the bunch. He said this always reminded him of when you were a boy—a teenager—I forget the exact word that he called it."

"Adolescence?"

"That's it. Adolescence. So much was happening to form and shape what you were going to be someday. Like the grape. I enjoyed listening to him think out loud because to him, the grape was a picture of each of our lives.

"During Stage Two, growth and visible change for the grape is slower, but a lot is happening that's unseen as the seeds continue maturing." Juan grinned. "Your father said this is the period of courtship, marriage, and family—the time when 'the bunch' is forming on the vine.

"And finally comes Stage Three. It begins with a sudden, dramatic change we call *véraison*. It's a time when growth speeds up again in what becomes the most crucial period of all for the grape. It's the time of 'final flavoring.' I'll tell you more about it later."

The three of them were quiet, eyes wandering over the silent, motionless, nearly naked vines that surrounded them.

"Do you hear it yet?" asked Juan.

Adam and Eva shook their heads.

"Hear what? What should we be hearing?" asked Adam.

Juan smiled and turned away. "I'll see you soon."

# *Véraison*

## VÉRAISON [Fr., pronounced vér-a-so]

(In order to maximize life's third and final developmental stage, the fifty-plus years, a series of "véraison" moments have been created to help you personalize, invigorate, and influence this exciting growth period in which you will shape the "final flavor" of your life.)

*Winter* seasons of the spirit often begin as drab, colorless periods during which one senses that the life force is draining away. We may feel driven back, hammered by problems or circumstances (i.e., forced retirement; the loss of a loved one; physical limitations).

1. Which, if any, of the following do you think applies to you right now?
   ☐ Feelings of dullness, lackluster, uninspired.
   ☐ Emotional detachment from people or circumstances.
   ☐ Disidentification through loss of a role or relationship.
   ☐ Old view was sufficient in the past, but not now.
   ☐ Confused, empty. The ordinary seems to possess an unreal quality.
   ☐ Continuing sense of dread or worry about the future.
   ☐ Uncertainty about job/company/career.

☐ Constantly busy but little to show for it.

☐ Sense of staleness in your marriage.

☐ Regret regarding important choices made earlier in life.

2. Be certain you understand that winter seasons of the spirit are times for—

REMINDING oneself of who you are;

RENEWING one's mission and purpose;

RESTORING one's physical and emotional energies;

REEVALUATING one's plans and goals;

RECHARGING the human spirit;

REJECTING defeatism.

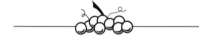

*"Think positively
about yourself,
keep your thoughts
and your actions clear,
ask God who made
you to keep
remaking you."*

—Norman Vincent Peale, late pastor
Marble Collegiate Reformed Church,
New York City, who believed that
***"one of the main tasks
of religion is to help people."***

The next day Juan did not come around. Adam and Eva walked alone in the vineyard, straining to hear something ... anything ... without success. It was the same the day after.

On the surface, nothing appeared to have changed. Yet, Adam did have to admit something was taking place, if only in his mind. For one thing, the more time he spent with them, the more the vines seemed to acquire personalities all their own. In jest, he even named a couple of the more recognizable ones "Frank and Ernest."

On day seven, they separated, each carrying a small folding stool and a water jug. At opposite ends of the field, they sat down and waited. An hour passed. Then another. And another. It was late in the afternoon when Adam caught sight of Eva waving excitedly. He gathered his things and went to her.

"I did it! I did it!" she exclaimed, hugging him enthusiastically. "I listened with my eyes!"

"And what did they hear?" Adam grinned dubiously.

Eva's expression was serene as she spoke the words softly, almost reverently.

"They heard the silence."

Adam looked steadily at Eva's face. She seemed so alive and vibrant, as though inspired by some great new awakening.

"You heard the silence?" he repeated at last.

"Yes. I was looking at these vines right here, letting my eyes follow along their different lines and shapes—thinking about what Juan said. It happened gradually, but I felt myself entering into a kind of inner quietness. There was such peace, Adam, I just can't tell you. And in this quietness the essence of the vines ... well, it was just there, that's all. First, I had this overwhelming impression of vitality and energy that just sort of exploded in my mind. And then I thought about death and rebirth."

"Easy now," cautioned Adam. "You're beginning to sound a little spacey, hon. You know, all that touchy feely 'at-one-with-the-earth-and-sky' sort of stuff? Too much meditating in the sun maybe?"

Calmly, she began again. "You know I'm not one for close encounters of a weird kind. I'm too down-to-earth for that. But I did think about death and rebirth. That's what these vines are engaged in right now, Adam. They've entered a season of deadness. They couldn't grow anything if they tried. Not anything worthwhile. The fascinating thing is, they seem to know that. So they just accept it. Surrender to it. And yet, in spite of outward appearances, they're not really dead. This is a time of emptiness between the old life and the new that's just part of their nature."

Adam stared at the nearest vines, gathering up what Eva was saying.

"You know what?" she asked.

"What?"

"I think this is some of what Dad wanted us to see and hear by staying close to the vineyard."

"Silence? Death and rebirth? That's pretty heavy stuff, Eva."

"I know. But look at us. We've been so busy tearing around from one thing to another that we're both exhausted. When we got news of Dad's condition, we were already running on the rims emotionally. We had depleted our inner resources. The difference is, we haven't had the sense to accept that. To surrender ourselves to it. We just keep on going and doing, even though our quality of life has been dropping off for some time. And think about Seth and Carrie. They've watched us long enough to believe that the way we've been living is natural."

"Well, isn't it?"

"You know what? I don't think it is. Or at least ... maybe ... it doesn't have to be."

"Really?"

"Yes, really. That's what I heard today. What do you think? Am I starting to listen with my eyes and see with my heart"?

Adam was silent. He saw something in her countenance—something familiar, yet changed in a way. Was it her eyes?

"Are you okay with that?" she asked finally.

"I'm not completely sure," Adam responded at last, "it's even a little scary. But, I think you're actually starting to make sense."

Eva poked him.

"Then maybe that's enough for one day," she said as they headed back toward the house. They walked in silence, arm in arm, until a slight smile crossed her face. Stopping she looked at Adam and said, "'What is best for man? That he should possess intellect. If he lacks intellect, then money so that he will be respected. If he has no money, then a wife who will conceal his faults. If he lacks a wife, then silence will hide his defects. And if he lacks silence, then the best thing for him is the grave.'"

"Whoa, where did that come from?"

"Hey, fella. I may be coming up on the big five-o in a couple of years, but I've got some smarts left. It's an old Hebrew saying my roommate taught me in college. I haven't thought about it for a long time. Until right now."

"Speaking of the big five-o, as you so delicately put it, I'm two months away from crossing over myself. Do you realize that?"

"As a matter of fact, I do," she smiled sweetly. "But not to worry. I've always loved older men."

"Fifty years old, two kids in college, and no job. Is it time to panic yet?"

"There's plenty of time for that tomorrow."

"And tonight?"

"Tonight? How about if I make us a cup of tea and we'll sit out here on the veranda, enjoy our winter view, and listen to the silence while the sun goes down. What do you say?"

Adam shuffled over to the railing and stared at the vineyard for a long moment. "What do you mean, 'winter view'?"

"Don't you remember when The Company transferred us down South? We went to look for a home and we kept seeing the phrase, 'winter view,' in the real estate listings. We couldn't figure out what in the world it was. Finally, we had to ask." Eva chuckled at the memory. "I think the realtor thought we were nuts. But, when he saw that we really didn't understand, he explained, 'In the summer, when the leaves are on the trees, all you can see are leaves.'"

"But in winter," Adam chimed in, "when the leaves are gone you get the big view. You can see all the way to the mountains! I remember now. It was so obvious that we'd missed it altogether."

He turned and faced Eva with a grin.

"So here we are listening to the silence and checking out the winter views. Sounds crazy, doesn't it? And yet I have a feeling we're about to make some discoveries we've not thought about before."

"Kinda fun, isn't it?" she said with an amused look as she patted his shoulder. Her tone impishly mocked that of a young woman in charge of a much older man. "Just sit here, sweetheart, and relax. You've not lost all your marbles yet. And, even if you do, I'll still love and take care of you, don't worry."

# *Véraison*

Winter views benefit the most when you:

1. <u>Specifically identify your winter storms.</u> The loss of a job, a friend, a mate. The pain of someone breaking your trust. Rejection. A period of loneliness or separation. A combination of these or other things. Whatever they are, see them. Walk around them in your mind. Give them a name. And know that they will not last forever.

2. <u>Embrace the winter's long darkness.</u> These are times for resting, restoring, "letting go," laying down weights from the past. Some winter weights to shed:
   - *Mad at God?* For bad "out-of-our-control" experences, some find it easiest to "blame God." Yet nearly four out of ten baby boomers turning fifty say that religion has become more important over the course of their lives as a source of community, spirituality, and solace.[4] Cultivate a positive spiritual side to your life.
   - *Hurt someone?* Offer a sincere apology. You'll make their day and your own too. When appropriate, volunteer restitution that leads to reconciliation (a face-to-face meeting, letter, monetary repayment, etc.). This is a weight you don't need to carry any longer. Get rid of it.

---

[4] Colm, Myles, *Our Boomers-Turning-Fifty Happiness Index*, New Choices. Feb. 1996, p. 27.

• *Been wronged or hurt?* Forgive. Do it without reservation. Even if it does not lead to restored relationships, the very act itself is a renewing force that helps us through our winter storms.

3. Discover winter's restorative power. Slow down. Way down! Take some time out. Listen to great music. Read a good book. This down time for your inner person is like watching snow fall, listening to the rain, feeling the warmth of a crackling fire.

4. Surrender to winter's barrenness. Accept it as one of life's normal rhythms. A time for discovery, not discontent. Delight, not discomfort. Resting instead of racing. A necessary time for restoring the body, soul, and spirit.

5. Understand that your winter seasons are gateways to new beginnings. They are essential to the wholeness and balance of your life. Surrender to their emptiness, to the process of disintegration and reintegration. The winter view is often the clearest view, something one can experience at no other time.

6. Let meditative moments be the warm spots in your winter seasons. Go to them daily. Mark out ten minutes. Then fifteen. Later, maybe half an hour.
   • Read inspiring, motivating books. Throw in a little poetry. Poetry can sometimes touch the human spir-

it like nothing else. Read the Bible. (If the Bible is a new idea to you, a helpful word: begin with a modern language version. Start with some of the great psalms. And the Gospel of Mark presents an eyewitness account of the life and teachings of Jesus, generally believed by scholars to have been recounted to Mark, in the main, by the Apostle Peter.)

- If you're married or have a roommate, read aloud to one another. Discuss what you've read, or simply sit back and enjoy.
- Spend time cleansing your mind of negativism, defeatism, all the liabilities. (One of the ways to accomplish this is to daily give thanks for health, family, and good friends, all the assets.)
- Don't stop until you are certain that you've counted and deposited more than enough assets to offset life's liabilities.

7. A succession of winter views over a lifetime is the best gateway to wisdom. *Give yourself permission to not produce during this season.* Concentrate instead on gaining perspective. We see the broader vistas through fields of naked, leafless branches. The ability to look at the "big picture" often provides insights for decision making that can be achieved in no other way.

The next day came and went. And the next. Soon a month had passed more quickly than either of them had at first thought possible. Winter's chill was in the air and cold rains made the hard ground soft underfoot. The weather shortened their daily visits to the vineyard, although their treks had become regular, almost habitual by this time. The morning hours were preferred. And the daily interval had brought about some definite changes.

At first, Adam felt silly sitting on a canvas stool, surrounded by grapevines, listening for "the silence." Anyway, all he could hear were cars in the distance, a train, and an occasional airplane overhead. His mind wandered, mentally checking off the things he should be doing: letters to write, phone calls to make, tasks concerning his father's estate, to name a few. His mind raced. He squirmed and glanced impatiently at his watch.

After several days, however, he began to relax. To concentrate on things close at hand. To feel the rhythms, to experience the natural integration of life's diverse elements, to eliminate the inconsequential, and indentify the important. And as he did, without at first realizing it, the silence drew nearer.

**Discovery.**             Bringing to light what was
hidden or forgotten.

**Meditation.**          To focus on; to reflect;
to ponder.

**Awareness.**           To realize; to perceive; to know
through experience.

### Interior Insight #2

Discovery + Meditation = Awareness.

# *Véraison*

Choose a place—your personal "vineyard"—where you can be alone with your own silence. Before proceeding further in the story, give a few minutes of thoughtful reflection to the following:

1. What hidden or forgotten place in my life would I most like to rediscover?_____

    _____

    _____

2. What part of my human existence do I most need to renew or refresh? _____

    _____

    _____

3. Am I aware of any rhythms—any flow or movement in my life—that are active at the moment? If so, what part of me is being affected (physical, emotional, spiritual)?_____

    _____

    _____

Is the overall effect largely
    ☐ positive  ☐ negative, or  ☐ a mixed bag?

4. What did I like/dislike the most about this time of silence?_____

    _____

    _____

hat had at first felt uncomfortably strange gave way eventually to a surprising emotional closeness with another world, one that he had not considered in a long time. The discordant noise of cars was erased by the silent movements of a jackrabbit whose curiosity, combined with Adam's acquiescence, permitted it to come closer each morning. The train's distant moan yielded to the determined rustling of breezes that caressed their way along each bare vine limb, offering nature's assurance that new life was coming. The faint sound of jet engines high in the sky was canceled by the nearer, more arresting call of wild geese passing low enough overhead that Adam could hear the steady beat of their wings.

But on one of his early morning forays, it occurred to him that things seemed out of place somehow. He was unsure of what it was exactly, and even more unsure of what to do about it. Still troubled that afternoon, he spied Juan walking along the far side of the field and went to him.

"Isn't there something we should be doing now?" Adam asked.

"Are you getting tired of 'listening'?" Juan grinned.

"Truthfully, no," Adam said, half surprised at his own admission. "The fact is, I now find myself looking forward to these quiet times. I've always thought I was too busy for this sort of thing. That it was an extravagance reserved for Eastern mystics or religious nuts while the rest of us were out conquering the world. But in this last month, I've seen and heard some things that I've never noticed before. I mean, nothing mystical—no close encounters or burning bushes. Just things that I'd never taken time to consider. They were always there, but I gave them no attention. No, I'm not planning on abandoning my early morning ritual, or whatever this is that I'm doing, but it does appear that there's work to do. Am I right?"

Juan nodded.

"Then what should I do first?"

"Watch me."

"Okay," Adam responded slowly, waiting for orders.

"No, I mean 'watch me,'" said Juan. "If you want to help the vines fulfill their purpose, you must watch me carefully. You have to learn the ways of the vines. If you do, you can develop the skills necessary to assist them. You see, out here, what's crucial is making certain that each vine has every opportunity to produce to its maximum capability. It's the most important thing. You and I are secondary. Our purpose is to help the vines be successful at what they do. If we accomplish that, we'll have achieved our purpose by helping them in theirs."

He paused. "Does that make sense?"

"I think so," Adam answered. "Actually, what you're saying is very much the same as where I work ... well, used to work. Those who supervise and manage are responsible for keeping The Company in good working condition, as well as for training and freeing the rest of the team to produce goods and sales. So here, it's a similar principle. We're the managers and supervisors and the vines are the production team."

"A good comparison," Juan agreed. "Here's another

way of looking at it. You and I are the parents. These vines are our children. They have no one else to care for them. If we don't, they'll grow up wild and unhappy and produce more bad fruit than good."

"The vines will be unhappy?"

"I know this may sound a little strange, but they understand their purpose in life. If they fail in it, they'll be unhappy," said Juan.

Adam stood silent, thinking.

"You know, these vines may be better off than me," he said at last, heaving a deep sigh. "I want to believe that my life is meaningful and that I have a real purpose. I thought I knew all that stuff. But since losing my job, and now my father, I'm beginning to wonder if I really know anything at all. How about you, Juan? Do you know what your purpose in life is?"

Juan let his gaze roam across the field before it returned to Adam.

"These vines," he answered firmly. "They are my purpose. I'm not a well educated man like you, Adam. I finished high school, that's all. But I know the vines. I'm gifted by God to take care of them. It's up to me to oversee the vineyard so that the vines can do their thing. Both they and I know this and we cooperate to make it happen. When we do, we're happy together."

"That's it then," said Adam. "That's what you do and you know you're in the right spot, so both you and the vines are a step ahead of me. You may not have as much education as you would have liked, yet you're a very wise individual. But who else are you, besides the vinekeeper? Who is Juan, the man? What's your passion—what are your dreams?"

Juan paused and, as Adam noted was the man's habit whenever he engaged in serious thinking, observed the ground by stirring it with the toe of his boot.

"I want to be a good man," he said quietly, looking up again. "I guess that's my 'passion,' as you call it. My wife doesn't have a perfect husband nor my children a perfect father, but I want them to know they have a good one. The best I can be. And someday ... I want to have my own vineyard."

"I've never asked you," said Adam, suddenly embarrassed at having been so self-absorbed with his own problems and personal quest that he had failed to do so. "How many in your family?"

"Rosa and I have three children."

"Where are they? Already gone from the nest?"

Juan seemed to grow taller as he answered, pride registered in his voice. "They're grown now. Alena works for an airline. Paulo is in college, a business major. Our oldest, Moises, works north of here in a vineyard, like his father, and lives at home to save money. So, at home, for now at least, it is the three of us."

"Have you ever wanted to do anything else?" Adam asked.

Juan shrugged. "This is what I know. It's my calling, my gift from God."

"What will happen to you if I sell the vineyard?"

Sadness fell like a shadow across Juan's face, then just as quickly, he brightened again. "I love this place as I loved your father. We were not just employer and employee. He was my best friend. He taught me many things, not just about the vines. I already knew most of the methods before coming here, and during my first years here I took some extension courses in viticulture at the community college. But he was my instructor in things I didn't know. He taught me to 'listen with my eyes and see with my heart.' The same things he wanted you to learn. I miss him. If the vineyard is sold, I will miss it as well. But, God has many other vineyards. And your father will always have a place in my heart."

That evening, when Adam returned to the house, he proceeded to help Eva prepare dinner. She had driven into town earlier to do some shopping and was interested to hear Adam recount his conversation with Juan.

"Do you think Juan would mind if I came with you to work tomorrow?"

"I asked him already," said Adam. "No problem. In fact, he seemed delighted that you might be there. One thing, though."

"What?"

"Don't forget your gloves," he said ruefully. "This working outdoors business is tough on hands."

# 1.

# Establish your personal meaning and purpose for life.

# *Véraison*

1. Our sense of meaning and purpose may need to change as we move through the stages of life. In fact, the journey into the fifty-plus years truly begins with that realization. Discuss with a spouse or close friend your reactions to the following:

- "We cannot live the afternoon of life according to the morning program." [5]
- Your feelings about running out of time in which to accomplish what is important.
- The possibility of redefining your sense of purpose as you approach and cross over the threshold of age fifty-plus.

2. Consider the question: *what am I going to do with the rest of my life?*
   In doing so, answer the following to the best of your ability:

- What is really important to me at this stage in my life?
- What new boundaries or limits will my answer require?
- Do you believe these things are also important to those who live with or around you?

3. Keeping in mind Interior Insight #2, *Discovery + Meditation = Awareness,* reflect on the events in your

---

[5] Manning, Brennan, *The Ragamuffin Gospel.* 1990. Multnomah Books, Sisters, Oregon, p. 165.

life (e.g., falling in love, birth of a child, death of someone dear, a personal spiritual experience). Which of these events do you think most helped to shape your current sense of meaning and purpose?

4. Describe in one sentence what you think the purpose of the Third Stage—the *véraison* stage—of your life might be. (Spend adequate time cultivating and refining your statement until it truly captures your sense of things.)

_____

_____

5. Recognizing that having a purpose in life may require acting "on purpose," list five specific things you intend to do on purpose to advance the cause of your life's meaning—beginning today:

(a)_____

(b)_____

(c)_____

(d)_____

(e)_____

*E* arly the next morning, Adam and Eva stood at the edge of the vineyard, gloves in hand, waiting for Juan to appear.

"Can you believe we've spent a whole month here already? Sitting in a vineyard? Listening to the silence? Checking out the 'winter view'? If the guys at work could only see me now."

Adam chuckled at the very idea.

"You know, I was just thinking how much of my identity has been tied up in that place. Most of my friends and a big percentage of our social life were centered around The Company. Now all of a sudden, that's gone. And for sure, once they pull you out of the lineup, you're out of the game! It's like we're here on some other planet, trying to figure out what happened. Trying to start over. Thank God I still have you!"

"And the kids. We still have Seth and Carrie. This really impacts all of us, Adam. There's been a lot of trauma for each of us to experience in such a little space of time."

"I guess that's true, isn't it?"

"Hey," exclaimed Eva, "I ran across something interesting yesterday. While you were out I found a book in your dad's library. He has some fascinating titles there. Have you noticed?"

Adam shook his head. "Dad's formal education was pretty limited, but he was always quite a reader. I just never paid much attention to what he read."

"Well, this one has been around for a while. It's called *The Ascetic Works of St. Basil.*"

"Mmm. Sounds like a real snoozer."

"It's actually quite interesting. There are some real similarities to what we've been doing these past weeks."

"No kidding?" Adam looked at her curiously.

"Yeah. This fellow, Basil, lived in the fourth century in what is now central Turkey. He studied at the University of Athens and was offered several opportunities for educational work. Instead, he decided to follow the ascetic and devotional life. Though it wasn't something he sought after or even wanted, he eventually became bishop of Caesarea, with a reputation as a warmhearted pastor who was genuinely concerned for the spiritual and physical well-being of his people."

"Sounds like a nice guy who would never get voted into public office today."

"What really interested me was that, as an ascetic, he spent a lot of time introducing and establishing the monastic system among the people of his day. Up to that time, ascetics had apparently lived in solitude or in groups of two or three. He changed that by forming several larger, self-sustaining 'communities.' In doing so, he really altered the entire outlook of ascetic life."

"And you somehow see that as akin to what we're doing here? We're about to qualify as monks, right?"

"No, silly," Eva laughed. "But you must admit to feeling a lot closer to God than you did a month ago."

Adam remained silent for a moment. Then his arm went around Eva and he drew her close.

"You're right. I've never been all that religious, as you

well know. Just a religious holiday kind of guy. None of it ever made that much of an impression, I guess. In all honesty, I suppose I never really felt like I needed it, so I never gave it a chance. But this ... " Adam let his eyes wander over the vineyard and then back to her, "this experience has been different, I'll have to admit."

"How so?"

"I've been asking myself that same question. I think I'm feeling like most of my life to this point has been spent acquiring stuff. Money, position, a good reputation, even my family—you and the kids."

"There's nothing wrong with that."

"No, I guess not. But our relationship has suffered at times as a result. I really regret that. I wondered if you were going to 'pull the pin' a few years ago. Remember?"

Eva nodded silently, thinking back to that lowest of moments in their marriage when she had questioned whether or not their life together was worth all the grief and distress she'd been feeling.

"I know I hurt you," Adam continued. "It wasn't intentional. I would never deliberately hurt you. It's just that I was awfully busy making a living, Eva."

"And?"

"And now I'm not sure that I know how to make a life."

They stood still for a long moment. Juan could be seen making his way toward them from the opposite end of the vineyard.

"Thank you," she said, reaching for Adam's hand.

"For what?"

"For telling me what it is you're feeling right now."

"You like hearing me fret over my worries and trepidations? I always thought you wanted emotional and material security from me."

"I do need those things," she replied. "But by sharing your feelings and your fears, you let me know that you trust me with them. I know that may sound convoluted to all your male 'protector instincts,' but you've just made me feel very secure emotionally. And look. We have an entire vineyard to work in today. It's all our own. So what more could we ask?"

"Well, for one thing, there's not a grape in the whole patch," he shrugged just as Juan came within earshot of their conversation.

"Prune them and they will come," Juan said with a smile as he took Eva's hand and turned it over in his, pretending to examine it carefully.

"Oh, now, this is the hand of a true viticulturist. I promise you that grapes will spring forth under the care of this hand." Then he looked at Adam's, pretending to examine it with great solemnity.

"This is a 'city hand' if ever I saw one," he pronounced at last, lifting it so that Eva could join him in a playful look. "Completely useless. See? There's no sign of this hand having ever worked before!"

The three of them broke out in laughter at Juan's good-natured teasing. Then they started into the vineyard.

# 2.

# Cultivate the sense of belonging, and nurture a few deeper relationships.

# *Véraison*

1. Write or call an old friend you haven't been in touch with for some time. Invest the effort to rekindle the relationship.

2. Make a list of all the people you would contact with news of unexpected joy (e.g., birth of a grandchild) or impending trouble (e.g., serious illness).

3. Do something radical. If it's been awhile (perhaps you've never done this before), say a simple prayer to acquaint or reacquaint yourself with God. (This is not a contest. God isn't awarding prizes for the best prayer offered up by our *Seasons* readers. And it has nothing to do with your religious background, or lack of it. (Just introduce yourself and explain honestly what you are thinking and feeling. If it's fitting, tell Him you're new at this, but that you'd like to do it more often from now on.)

4. Make a new friend. Speak to a person you see at the supermarket. Sit in another spot at your place of worship. Join in activities there. Or volunteer in a political organization's cause that interests you. Remember, many of the best and most interesting friendships are the byproduct of a mutual interest or activity.

5. Have you written or placed a call of reconciliation yet to someone from whom you've been estranged? Rid yourself of this "winter weight."

   Express your regret and your desire to be forgiven for your contribution to the estrangement. (Before you make the contact, ask God to prepare that person to receive your message of good will.) Don't forget to say the words, "Will you forgive me?" (This is also a good way to deal with one's feelings of personal estrangement from God.)

The work was hard and it wasn't long before a cool sweat began trickling into Adam's eyes. He glanced over at Eva. Her countenance was pleasant, with just the trace of a smile warming her features. Though the temperature was bracing, and gray clouds were threatening to move in front of the sun by midday, she seemed to be thoroughly enjoying herself.

The three of them spent the morning walking each row, gathering rubbish, leaves, shriveled overlooked grapes, and broken branches left from the harvest. Adam didn't complain about the mundane assignment. He actually felt exhilarated by the physical labor and his inclusion in something out of the ordinary. He could see where they had been. He liked that. It was altogether different than spreadsheets or appointment calendars. The key to the feeling of fulfillment was in the difference they were making. It wasn't exactly earthshaking or life-changing, but it felt good. Really good!

At noon, Eva asked Juan to join them for lunch at the house. At first he hesitated, until receiving repeated assurances that his presence would not be a burden. When the three of them were seated around the table, Adam reached for the sandwich plate.

"Dig in," he encouraged, passing the plate to the others.

"If you're not too tired, I'll show you how we prune the vines this afternoon," Juan said.

"Oh yes, we'd like that," Eva responded. "It's been great fun doing something constructive this morning."

"You understand we know nothing about this,"

Adam admitted. "I'd hate to cut off the wrong branches. I mean, we're talking about living things here."

"Oh, they're 'living things' now, are they?" Juan repeated with a puckish grin. "A few weeks ago I seem to recall they all looked dead to you. So this is good. You're beginning to form a relationship with the vines, no?"

"Well, I'm not sure I'd use the word 'relationship,'" answered Adam, "but I have made a few new acquaintances out there. When we go out again, would you like me to introduce you to Frank and Ernest?"

| | |
|---|---|
| **Necessity.** | The pressure of our circumstances. |
| **Competence.** | The abilities or qualities that enable a response. |
| **Accomplishment.** | The desired result brought about through effort; to make a difference. |

## Interior Insight #3

Necessity + Competence = Accomplishment.

*W*hat's involved in your annual work program in this vineyard?" Eva inquired as they were walking back to the field, still uncomfortable at the thought of calling it "our" vineyard.

"The same as in all vineyards," Juan answered. "There are some differences, of course, depending on the type of grape that's planted, soils, moisture, temperature, whether the land is flat or hilly. That sort of thing. But, basically, it begins here with an ending."

"Did you say an ending? Doesn't everything start at the beginning?"

Juan smiled understandingly. "Not with nature. Harvest is over and the grapes are in the hands of the winemakers. Here, as you can see, weeds continue to grow, but in general, the vines themselves are dormant. This is their time to restore and renew. What we call 'leaf fall' happens, and we begin pruning. As you've already seen, it's not a very upbeat time. Things look pretty jumbled and wasted. But this is one of the most important periods in the life of the vine."

Adam nodded. "You know, when we first arrived here, I didn't like what I saw. It reminded me so much of what I was feeling in my own life at the time. It's been several years since Mom passed away, of course, but Dad's dying opened up that whole emptiness again. And to be honest, saying good-bye to my friends at The Company the way I did felt pretty humiliating. I guess I was identifying with the deadness I saw around here. But I'm starting to appreciate the difference between dead and dormant, and the fact that these vines aren't really dead at all. And maybe ..." he paused and looked across the field.

"And maybe what, dear?" asked Eva gently, sensing her husband's pensive mood.

" ... maybe I'm not 'dead' yet either. Maybe all this hasn't happened by accident. Maybe this is really a time that was meant to be. To force us to redefine and renew what we're about."

Eva slipped her arm through his, saying nothing and yet saying everything.

"God is at work in everything to bring about our good," Juan commented, a pleased look on his face. "He even works in the things that seem bad at the time. You know, I think you are beginning to 'hear with your eyes and see with your heart.'"

Then he turned away to the field. "But right now we should get to work. Those clouds are going to get us wet before I can make expert pruners out of you."

## *Véraison*

1. Look back over the last ten years. Notice and name any aspects of your life you recognize as having been "pruned away" during that stretch of time. Ask yourself:

   (a) Am I stronger as a result?_____

   _____

   _____

   (b) Do I still bear the "scars"?_____

   _____

   _____

   (c) Which of the pruned away shoots have tried to reappear?_____

   _____

   _____

2. What "pruning" experiences do you see ahead of you? Are there any preparations you can make to better cooperate with the "Pruner" in the future?

   _____

   _____

3. Our personal sense of purpose is driven, in part, by a feeling of confidence in being able to do some-

thing well (e.g., cooking, bookkeeping, making and sustaining friendships, memorizing poetry).

Name three "competencies" that you've developed to this point in your life:

(a) _____

(b) _____

(c) _____

Now, list three "competencies" you would like to add to your life (noting, as you do, what steps you can take to make them happen):

(a) _____

(b) _____

(c) _____

*O*kay, look around you," said Juan as they stood in one of the rows separating the vines. "If these vines were growing in a natural setting, they would have to compete with trees, shrubs, and various plants for light, water, and other nutrients. But it would be at a distinct disadvantage. As you can see, it doesn't have a thick trunk to hold it up, so it has to manage in different ways. Its tendrils clasp onto neighboring branches and climb upward."

"I would think the opposite to be true," said Adam. "If soil conditions were perfect, then the vines should be perfect too."

"Good soil and excellent conditions can certainly result in good vines. But just because conditions are less than perfect is no excuse for the vine. It simply has to work harder and dig deeper. Ask yourself—if drought or storm or any other adversity becomes a factor in the vineyard, which vine will be the last to go?"

Adam and Eva nodded their silent understanding.

"So that's why the trellis system is used in the fields? To provide a supporting structure?"

"Exactly. It's an alternative that the vinekeeper must provide because the field is not a natural setting."

"A kind of 'support group' for grapevines," Eva commented.

"Yes, and while it grows very rapidly in the spring and summer seasons, it's important to its survival to develop a vigorous root system that goes deep into the soil looking for water and nutrients. The poorer the soil and the drier the summer, the deeper the roots must go."

"I guess that's what Alex Haley was trying to say when he wrote the book *Roots*," Adam commented.

"Another thing that's interesting is the lack of competition," added Juan. "Look around you."

Their eyes slowly moved across the field.

"This is a 'monoculture.' Your father helped me understand this. The only contesting here is with neighboring grapes. The tendency, then, is for excessive growth to occur, almost as though one vine tries to outdo the others."

"Keeping up with the Joneses?" smiled Adam.

"In a manner of speaking. But all this excessive growth has very little value. So the vines need help to save them from their own natural tendencies. That's where we come in. We act as agents of control. In fact, every winter we customarily remove ninety percent of the canes from the previous season, along with a certain amount of summer growth."

"Ninety percent?" repeated Adam incredulously. "I hadn't imagined so much!"

"It's necessary," said Juan. "If constant pruning didn't occur, the vines would lose sight of their purpose and attempt to overpower one another. Ultimately, there would be only a tangled mess."

"Reminds me of living in The City," Eva commented dryly. Adam chuckled his agreement.

"Pruning has several purposes," continued Juan. "We want to space the shoots so that each will offer its leaves adequate sunlight during the growing season. Air circulation is important too, helping to lower the negative effect of humidity. It also allows for better pest and disease control, provides good replacements for the next winter's pruning, and gives the buds the best opportunity for fruiting."

"So the better the job done during the winter season while there's opportunity for pruning, the better the chances for the vine to do its thing through the rest of the year," said Adam. "It's just hard to stand here and imagine we're doing the vines a favor by cutting and trimming away all they've worked so hard to put forth during the last growing season. It doesn't seem ... normal somehow."

"It's very normal," Juan said reassuringly. "In fact, it's normal for every living thing that wants to thrive and achieve and be healthy."

"It's just that, living in today's world as we do," Eva broke in, "the emphasis in society seems always to be on getting more and growing bigger, not trimming and cutting back. I think that's what Adam is saying."

"But are we healthier for it?" asked Juan. The others were silent. "One of your father's favorite sayings about tending the vines was that 'more' is not necessarily 'better.' And when we listen to the vines, this is part of what they tell us. The most productive living things are fearless when it comes to cutting away and pruning back nonessentials. It's not a matter of outgrowing their neighbors. It's a matter of living in harmony together. When this happens, it makes it possible for all to achieve their maximum potential. And when that takes place the whole field prospers."

"At what point do you stop pruning?" queried Adam, running his gloved hand along the roughness of a leafless branch.

"During winter, of course, is when the major pruning is done. But there always seems to be a need for more. In summer, it depends on the vigor of the vines. If it's low, once or twice will suffice. If there's a great deal of vitality, maybe three or four times. The key idea during the Summer Season is to avoid excessive pruning, always working with an eye to increasing the number of fruitful buds. Normally, especially in cooler areas like this, the growth of shoots decreases when the grapes are in their final stage. This means that the last pruning will normally take place sometime around véraison."

"Véraison?" Eva questioned. "You mentioned that word earlier when you were talking about the stages of a grape's life."

"Yes. Véraison is the beginning of the third stage—the last phase of grape growth, the time when the final flavor is being formed. Then comes harvest! Adam's father used to say this is what happens to humans at midlife."

The three stood silently for a moment, surveying their bleak, seemingly lifeless surroundings. It was all so hard to imagine.

"There's a verse from the Bible your dad liked to quote," Juan continued. "'Whatever your hand finds to do, do it with all your might, for in the grave, where you are going, there is neither working nor planning nor knowledge nor wisdom.'"[6]

"That's what my doctor says. Keep working and stay young. I'm sure that Dad's work kept him younger in body

---

[6] The Bible. Ecclesiastes 9:10.

and spirit." Adam wiped his gloves against his pants as he glanced at Eva. "And what pearl of wisdom are you about to add to this humble little collection?"

"Some people pray for more things than they're willing to work for," she said.

The men laughed.

"Enough talk," Juan declared, turning toward a nearby vine. "Now we go to work. Let me show you how it's done."

For the next hour, he patiently explained and demonstrated where the cuts should be made. He watched Adam and Eva follow his example, cautioning when he saw them start to make an imprudent cut, praising when they did it right. It was slow at first and both of them were a bit nervous, having never done anything like this before.

Gradually, however, they fell into a purposeful rhythm. And there were fewer and fewer criticisms of their work from Juan. In fact, once he was assured of their understanding, he turned away and began working in the row next to theirs. His pace was much swifter than Adam and Eva. His practiced skill allowed him to do more than both of them put together and, now and then, he paused to revisit what they were doing, pointing out any incorrectness while, at the same time, lauding their fledgling proficiencies.

By the time the first drops of rain were felt, the sun was barely visible, low on the gray horizon. The afternoon was almost spent. They paused briefly to look back along the rows in which they had done their "winter work." Dead leaves and cuttings lay strewn about on the damp earth. The vines themselves appeared clean and trim. Adam and Eva smiled at each other and resumed their tasks, just as the rain began coming down in earnest.

"Let's call it a day," Juan said, as he walked toward them. Try as they might, they had been no match for his swift and efficient work. He had spent no small amount of time coaching and critiquing their efforts while still accomplishing twice what the two of them had done together.

"How do you do it?" asked Adam admiringly, looking at the area in which Juan had been working.

Juan shook his head as if to fend off any intended compliment. "You must remember that caring for the vines is God's gift to me. Not everyone has such a gift. You? We'll wait and see. We're all like these vines, created to blossom and bear fruit. The difference is that while the grapevine understands its purpose, we humans must discover ours."

"What do you mean?" inquired Adam.

"Can I try to answer that?" Eva interrupted before Juan could respond. Juan nodded, motioning with his hand for Eva to go ahead.

"I think what Juan means is that we each are given different skills to be developed and gifts to be discovered at the outset of our existence. When we understand and accept what these are and begin to express them fully, then our highest purpose as human beings can be realized in what we do and in what sort of person we become."

"You're 'seeing with your heart,'" complimented Juan as the three of them gathered up their tools and began walking in the direction of the house. "Once we enter into the rhythm of life that comes from this discovery, we are happy and fulfilled."

The rain was coming down steadily as they neared the edge of the field.

"I'll let you go," said Juan. "Rosa will have dinner ready before too long. You've done a good day's work. Even you, Adam, with your 'city hands.' Enjoy the rest of your day."

"These 'city hands' are looking forward to some warm water and a peaceful, quiet evening," Adam answered with a rueful grin. "They may never be the same again!"

# *Véraison*

Realizing that "to belong" is a prerequisite to happy living, create a sociogram that portrays your network of friendships:

• List each social group you are a part of, the ones in which the people know you by name. Examples: immediate family, extended family, work or recreational groups (teams, friends from the job), religious organizations (choirs, committees, study groups), service/civic groups, etc.[7]

• Now rate each group on a scale of 1-5
(1 = lowest; 5 = highest) on the effectiveness
with which it

    (a) makes you feel that you are a valued member;

    (b) gives you a sense of purpose in your life;

    (c) contributes to your overall happiness.

| GROUP | FEELING OF VALUE | SENSE OF PURPOSE | HAPPINESS |
|---|---|---|---|
|  |  |  |  |
|  |  |  |  |
|  |  |  |  |
|  |  |  |  |
|  |  |  |  |

---

[7] As lifelong associations with business firms and corporations decrease, so does the influence of these organizations in providing a source for lasting relationships.

*A*fter the dinner dishes were washed and put away, Adam and Eva stood on the veranda once again, steam rising from mugs filled with tea that were balanced on the railing in front of them. The rain was beginning to let up as darkness settled around them. A yellow ribbon of car lights could be seen in the distance. Adam stared silently into the gathering night.

"What are you thinking, dear heart?" asked Eva, her voice soft and loving as she rested her hand on his.

"How lucky I am to be married to you," he replied.

"That's the right answer," she declared sweetly, looking up at him.

"And how good it felt to work in the vineyard today."

"You liked it?"

"Yes. In some ways it was even exhilarating. I liked being able to see what we accomplished. I can't say that pruning will ever be my 'gift,' as Juan calls it, but I have to admit that I enjoyed the feeling of working with living things that accept correction even when it's painful. When you think about it, those vines are truly amazing. It's like they all get along beautifully. They just want to produce fruit, that's all. It's too bad it wasn't more like that at The Company. For that matter, it's too bad it's not more like that in The World. It could be, you know."

"That's a wonderful thought, Adam. Everybody living out their lives in utter selflessness. I guess it's true that when we 'live to give' we're the happiest. Do you think it will ever happen?"

"I don't know. Maybe that's part of my problem,"

Adam mused thoughtfully, sipping from the mug as he leaned back against the railing. "I'm almost fifty years old and it feels as though most of my life has been spent gathering instead of giving."

"Look at it this way, love," Eva countered. "So far, you've been a great husband and father. You've given yourself to make us a life. Were there nothing else, this alone should provide you with a sense of accomplishment."

"But the kids are grown now, or at least almost. Anyway, they're pretty well headed out on their own. For all intents and purposes, it's just us now."

"And that bothers you?"

"No. Of course not. I didn't mean for it to sound that way. Actually, I'm looking forward to the 'empty nest.' I love the kids, but to have just you and me again—by ourselves—the way it was when we were first in love."

"With a few wrinkles and love-handles added here and there," Eva smirked playfully, pinching his waist. Adam laughed.

"Yes, I guess we can never really go back, can we?" he mused, slipping his arm around her. "Only forward. But, forward to what?"

"How about to véraison?"

"To what?"

"Véraison. The 'third stage,' that Juan was talking about. The final flavoring of our lives. You know, I really like the sound of that. I've been thinking—this ought to be the best part of our lives coming up, right? It's the first opportunity we've had since we were kids ourselves to plan for our future again. And I'm not talking about security alone."

"Then what?"

"Do you remember those walks along the lake when we used to dream about our future? About what we were going to do with our lives? Well, think about it, Adam. We've done most of those things. At least the important ones. Our list is pretty well used up."

"Maybe it's more than the list that's used up," Adam lamented.

"No. That's just it. We've got time. We've got our health, thank God. And we have each other. What we don't have is 'direction.' And that's something we really need now. So I was thinking. How have we found our way in the past? It's often been our relaxed and meditative moments that have resulted in the most creative insights. We're like an old grandfather clock—still ticking, but not for much longer unless somebody pulls our chain because the same 'weights' that keep us ticking, left unattended, are the ones that ultimately drag us down."

Eva turned to look directly at Adam.

"Wouldn't it be wonderful if we could produce something so valuable that it would last long after we're gone?" she continued. "In a way, you were right when you said we've spent most of our lives 'gathering,' but I don't think that's negative at all. So far life has been a great classroom for us. We've gathered skills and wisdom along the way. Now it's time to prune whatever we've accumulated that's meaningless and burdensome in order to produce our most fruitful and fulfilling years.

"Giving something back. For some reason, that seems really important to me right now. Not simply things, or our finances for the kids to divvy up, but a piece of ourselves. Painting life a more brilliant color just because we can! What do you want to do, Adam?"

"I'm not exactly sure, but I know this much. I don't believe I'll ever be satisfied again to just punch in and out of life's time clock. Accumulating things is not nearly as important to me now as it was a few months ago." Adam swallowed the last of his tea before continuing. "The thought of ever really making a difference in the world through what I might have to offer has always seemed too fanciful and transcendental to me. At least until now. Now, I keep thinking of those vines out there. They understand what their purpose is and fulfill it without question. They relate to each other in positive, reinforcing kinds of ways. And they know they'll all make a contribution. There's something inside me that wants to be like that."

# 3.

Make
an
effective
and
useful
contribution.

*"I am a little pencil in the*

*hand of a writing God*

*who is sending a love letter*

*to the world."*

—Mother Teresa, founder,
The Order of the Missionaries of Charity. Her
devotion to the destitute earned her the Nobel
Peace Prize in 1979.

# *Véraison*

*Spring* seasons of the spirit are times of personal awakening, of fresh, new discovery about oneself. We recognize within us the regaining of excitement, expectancy. Something is about to happen, but what? Ideas and long-held dreams swell like bud burst with the promise of fruitfulness and adventure.

1. Which of the following do you think send the most important signals regarding the coming of spring to your own inner spirit? (Choose five in order of priority).

☐ A "feeling" that the current state of dormancy through which I've been living is almost over.

☐ Excitement about the future.

☐ Breaking down my limited view of things.

☐ A fresh appreciation of time.

☐ An invigorating love for the ordinary.

☐ Creative energy.

☐ A new understanding of the importance of solitude.

☐ "PMA" = positive mental attitude.

☐ The renewed cultivation of my "inner environment."

☐ Desire to be self-employed.

☐ Reaching out to others and being enriched in the process.

☐ Sharing the wisdom of experience with the young.

☐ Leaving behind an improved natural environment.

☐ Having someone to emulate at this time in my life.

2. List the names of five people to whom you would like to express appreciation for what they've done or to affirm their giftedness. (If you need some help "priming the pump," create your own variations from these samples):

_____

_____

_____

_____

_____

(a) "I'm lucky to be married to you!"
(b) "I enjoy watching someone with your talent do your thing.'"
(c) "I appreciate all you do to ... "
(d) "You're one of the best _____ I've ever ... "
(e) "Never let anyone tell you that you can't; I think you're terrific!"
(f) "Thanks for what you said the other day."

3. Name some people who've helped to "flavor" your

life. What sort of "flavorings" have they added?

_____

_____

_____

_____

_____

4. Review again your responses to the sociogram exercise. Select the names of three people in your circle of relationships for whom you would like to be a "source of flavor" during the next few months/years. Identify the first steps you'll take to make this happen.

| NAMES | FIRST STEPS |
|-------|-------------|
|       |             |
|       |             |
|       |             |
|       |             |

*Emerging growth*
*is an unstoppable*
*sequence*
*requiring routine,*
*yet indispensable*
*work.*
*It is humankind's*
*litany*
*celebrating*
*the Spring Season.*

*D*uring the following weeks, at the end of each long workday, Adam and Eva mulled over the state of things, taking more time to dream and talk about their future than they had in years. Adam felt himself being drawn to Eva with a growing revitalization. Eva enjoyed the sense of being nurtured and enriched by the deepening of their relationship. In fact, she could not remember a time in which she had felt any more in love and committed to her husband than right now.

"We're like a couple of kids again," Eva declared late one evening, her face aglow in the candlelight.

"Better than kids," Adam responded as she laid her head on his chest. The soft scent of her perfume and the smell of freshly washed hair filled him with sweet memories. Days and nights when they had been there for each other just like this—before parenting and career-carving had consumed their every waking hour.

Position.

Power.

Possessions.

Adam had begun questioning the importance of these factors in his life. At first it had been confusing. Even upsetting. The absence of two of the most familiar pieces of the life he'd been living—his job and his father—had become blended with new pieces. The vineyard. Juan. Even Eva, seen now in a new light that initiated subtle shifts and changes in his thinking.

What did it all mean?

He was discomfited over the growing recognition that

many years had passed during which he'd failed to honor and affirm Eva with respect to her gifts and skills—even her own personhood. Her contribution to their lives had often gone ignored and outwardly unappreciated. He knew he'd taken for granted the fact that she was always there for him. Now, he wasn't sure how she felt about it, but he was determined to ask when the time was right.

He had to admit that he'd also neglected putting much effort into building true friendships—effort that expressed genuine interest in others without attaching ulterior expectations or demands. Even his relationships with Seth and Carrie had been on "remote control" much too long. He vowed to invest more of himself—his time, attention, energies, and service—in all the important interpersonal connections in his life. Adam was determined to do things differently—beginning now—at life's midpoint.

The winter holidays with the children came and went.

It was a cheerful time, the happiest that any of them could remember, lifting all of their spirits. Both Seth and Carrie seemed to be doing well in college. Especially Seth. Eva's thirty-seven-year-old unmarried sister had agreed to live with their children during the remainder of the school year. She joined with them in celebrating the holidays.

During the two weeks they spent together at the vineyard house, Adam and Eva marveled at their children's energy and enthusiasm, as sonorous and vibrant as ever. Yet this year it seemed muted at times by some undefinable, overshadowing presence. What was it? The blossoming of a new maturity perhaps? Or signs of an impatient breaking away? Was it concern over an uneasy armistice as time for the final surrender of parental control drew nearer? Or perhaps a sense of mourning over the disconcerting worldliness that appeared to be displacing the innocent, puerile charm of their youth?

Eva shared her feelings with Adam and they wondered what would finally become of these two cuttings from their own branches. For Seth and Carrie, it seemed, the last winter of parent-pruning was nearly over. They laughed as they remembered how it had been for themselves at that age. So much to be. So much to do. So much to learn.

"When we were young and impetuous," Adam recalled, "we faced life with all the untested fearlessness of first-time climbers, ready to tackle a high mountain. We had no clue as to the sacrifice and pain involved in the climb, but we had this incredible confidence. We knew we could do it if given the chance."

"And we did do it, didn't we?" Eva responded, gathering inner solace from the shared memories.

"Yes, we did," answered Adam. "There were a few unanticipated missteps, some cuts and scrapes, and a couple of bad spills, but we did it. And they will too."

While reminiscing, the conversation drifted away from the children to their own renewed sense of closeness and well-being—on feeling as relaxed and robust as they had in years. They agreed that it was not just a "feeling," however. It was a fact. As a result of working every day in the vineyard their bodies had grown firm and indefatigable.

The vineyard's major pruning season was over. Limbs,

leaves, and weeds had been cleared away. Broken trellises had been repaired or replaced, depending on the need. The vines appeared as bare as sheep fresh from the shearing sheds. Stripped of yesterday's glory. More gaunt and naked than ever.

And yet a serene expectancy hovered over the vineyard. An elegant silence, like that of a woman awake at night, feeling the movement of her unborn child stirring within. Adam and Eva sensed it each morning as they walked among the rows. It was the promise of things hoped for but as yet unseen. The vines were silently becoming pliant and malleable, sleek and ready to give birth once again.

One morning, the three of them stopped in front of a particular vine. "Come close," urged Juan. "Look at this." Adam and Eva closed in around him to see. He brushed his fingers back and forth over a section of the branch.

"See how it's swelling?" He held the branch out so that the others could see. "Soon it will be 'bud burst.'"

An air of excitement continued to build as each day added new minutes of sunlight and temperatures warmed with the advent of spring. Juan became more animated, a new energy evident in his steps and demeanor. The same was true for Adam and Eva as well, but for different reasons.

The weeks had become months following the passing of Adam's father and those first bleak days of wandering through the vineyard in search of a promise in which they did not really believe.

With the approach of spring, those cheerless days were

but a memory. Now the vines spoke quite often. Almost daily, it seemed, new lessons were being taught that applied to their lives. Adam and Eva were improving the skills of "listening with their eyes and seeing with their hearts." The old man's riddle was no longer a mystery.

"I can see it so clearly now," exclaimed Eva one day. "Why couldn't I see it before?"

"Because we were still in life's 'fast lane,'" Adam responded, "busy trying not to get run over. I thought Dad simply wasn't thinking clearly at the time. But it wasn't him at all. He was clear as a bell. It was us. He knew that the vines could only 'communicate' through the eye-gate. Without words, the only way to 'hear' what they have to tell us is with our eyes."

"And the only way to truly see," added Eva, "is by building a bridge of understanding that passes through the vines and into our hearts. Adam, the more I think about it, the more I realize what a wise and loving man your father was. He wasn't just a grape grower. He invested himself in us both—and we're just now seeing the 'bud burst' that's the result of his efforts!"

As daylight hours drifted into pristine, unspoiled evenings, they discussed the things they had "seen" and "heard." Sharing inner thoughts and feelings had become an important part of their day. Because they were at work in the field early each morning, the sunset hours had come to be their special time for sharing a warm tea or a cool drink, to recall the day's events, and to discuss an insight or a discovery that had stirred their spirits along the way.

Every evening, Adam looked with pride at the rows stretching away from the house, each one pruned and every row raked clean. Then one day, an idea formed in his mind. He asked Juan about planting grass along the rows, indicating that he thought it would make work more pleasant with a carpet of green to walk or kneel on.

Juan listened patiently until Adam had finished. Then he explained that in some cooler, damper climates where heavy rains might wash away quantities of soil on slopes, or where it could aid with rapid moisture penetration in flat areas, it was sometimes considered advantageous to do so. In this region, however, clean-cultivation was preferred, causing the soil to lose less moisture than if covered by weeds or grasses.

He pointed out that because there is less humidity over bare ground, fungus rots are discouraged. Bare ground also absorbs more heat during the day and releases it at night. Grass, on the other hand, requires a good deal of extra maintenance. And, because grasses and weeds compete with the vines for nutrients, there are usually more nutrients available to the vines on soil that is clean-cultivated.

"Have you ever noticed how hard we work for things that we think will enhance or beautify our lives?" Adam asked that evening, after telling Eva of Juan's response to his earlier idea, while sitting together on the veranda. "Yet, sometimes ... in the long run ... their inclusion takes our attention away from what really matters."

"Beauty and comfort do offer things important to life's enrichment," Eva responded, "but I guess we need to consider carefully whether or not they'll ultimately enrich or take away from our truly important goals."

"Yeah. Like the time I bought that new car right after we were engaged—remember?"

"How could I forget. We drove away from our wedding reception in real class, that's for sure."

"And then we struggled to make the payments while trying to stay in school at the same time."

"Yep. I also remember the night we decided it was the car or college. Trading down to that old Plymouth was humbling."

"It was indeed. But we made the right choice."

"Yes, we did," admitted Eva, her eyes reflecting the images of a distant memory come close. "One that respected and affirmed each other and our life goals instead of an inanimate object."

Adam chuckled. "It was a benchmark decision for a couple of young kids. Buy down and stay in school. Looking back, it seems silly that it was so hard to do."

"Sometimes it takes courage to correct a wrong choice with a right one. Especially one as visible to your friends as a new car."

| | |
|---|---|
| **Experience.** | To observe, participate in, and learn from the events that make up one's life. |
| **Choice.** | Possessing the power to select freely and, after consideration, to decide. |
| **Wisdom.** | To be able to discern inner qualities and relationships and to determine sound courses of action based on one's choices and experience. |

### Interior Insight #4

Experience + Choice = Wisdom.

# *Véraison*

1. List five key "lessons of life" that you have learned over the years. As you list them, put a check beside the ones that resulted from difficulty or some painful experience. Place a "star" beside the ones that, if shared, could conceivably be a source of encouragement to others.

   (a) _____

   (b) _____

   (c) _____

   (d) _____

   (e) _____

2. How might you contribute to the possibility of "bud burst" in someone with whom you are closely associated?

   _____

   _____

3. Make a list of specific words/phrases or actions with which you could affirm and encourage the production of fruit in others.

   _____

   _____

   _____

   _____

# 4.

Give and
receive
affirmation
and respect.

The following day, Adam and Eva became witnesses to the onset of a miracle. The vineyard had begun birthing its children. The long period of dormancy had finally broken!

As temperatures warmed, the swelling buds burst with the emergence of tiny shoots. Juan cautioned that the shoots were soft and tender and susceptible to frost. He made certain that giant fans, as tall as a house, were made ready to move the air throughout the vineyard and help negate the effects of any cold spring night.

"So what happens now?" asked Adam, feeling very much like a new father.

"This is a time to watch and be ready," answered Juan. "The buds are beginning to form in the axils of the leaves. As the shoots develop, each bud will divide into two, one remaining dormant until next spring, while the other forms a lateral shoot. In the dormant bud two smaller ones will develop, one of which will burst the following year. And so it goes on and on."

"I guess nature takes its course from here on then. What do we do? Coast the rest of the way to harvest?"

"No, it's not that easy," Juan continued. "Although it's true that the growing season is in many ways a 'coasting' period, the vineyard is still very dependent upon the vinekeeper. If the nights become too cold, as may very well happen during the spring season, it's up to us to provide a temporary atmosphere that will protect and preserve the vines. And there is still pruning to be done, though not of the radical nature required during winter.

"We have to strip away the excessive vegetative growth or the development of flower initials in the buds will be hampered. But it has to be done carefully so as not to remove large areas of mature leaves. That would prove equally detrimental. Flower initiation is promoted by high light intensity. That's why this is so important. The amount of light that touches the developing bud is critical.

"This is a period during which we must carefully strike a balance between the work of the Creator and that of the caretaker. Some things only God can do and some we must do for ourselves. Where we often have difficulty in the vine-yard is in failing to remeber which is which."

Adam and Eva listened intently.

"This is a lot like parenting, isn't it?" Eva concluded at last.

"Or being parented," said Juan. "Perhaps this is why children are sometimes called the 'fruit of their mother's womb.' Anyway, you see again the undeniable connection between the vine, the vinekeeper, and the Creator. It's a per-petual bond that must not be broken through carelessness or neglect."

"Interdependency," Eva mused, "between the Seen and the Unseen. Each needs the other."

"Exactly. Any breakdown in this relationship can only bring about harmful results. The vine is helpless without a constant positive interaction with the surrounding elements of nature—sunlight, water. Nutrients from the soil. Even the wind is important to its conservation."

"You mean to reduce the risk of frost-kill?"

"That's part of it, but there's much more. Now that it's spring, you can see the buds appearing. After the buds burst, leaves will follow, but the flowers themselves will not open for another six or eight weeks. Each flower wears a tiny cap and when anthers are ready to be released the cap is doffed and the pollen from the anthers falls on the stigma."

"That's something I haven't thought about in a long time. You sound like my professor in Biology 101."

Juan grinned and nodded his head.

"We call it capfall. But here's the thing about the wind. Grapevines are different from many plants in that they're not dependent on bees or any other insects to spread the pollen. What's needed are a few warm, dry days and some light winds. It's almost as though God decided not to rely on anything or anyone but Himself to insure the propagation of grapes."

"Well, they say that Jesus turned water into wine at a wedding," Eva smiled. "So I guess the grapes must be important to Him."

"Vineyards have been around for many centuries. Noah was a sailor only by necessity," Juan reminded them with a smile. "He was actually a 'man of the soil.' As the story goes, one of the first things he did after the Flood was plant a vineyard. Unfortunately, one of the things he did soon after that was get drunk."

"Confirms the old saying, 'anything worth doing is worth overdoing,'" Adam said with an amused chuckle.

"In the mountains of Iran," Juan continued, "scientists recently found the oldest evidence to date for wine in some residue at the bottom of a 7,000-year-old pottery jar. This jar may even be older than Noah."

"Now that's what I call aging the wine!" exclaimed Eva. "But finish telling us about the growth cycle."

"Yes. Well, following capfall, in two or three days the fertilization process is complete. In another two or three days the flowers that, for whatever reason, are still unfertilized begin dropping off—we call that shatter. The flowers that are fertilized and remain on the bunch have set.

"As I've mentioned before, after flowering and set, the growth of the grape occurs in three stages. There's an initial period of rapid growth, followed by a second phase that's much slower. Then comes véraison and the third stage, the final growth period. When véraison takes place, the growth is sudden and very dramatic.

"The berry begins to soften, acidity decreases, while glucose and sucrose increase. In the red and black varieties of grapes, this is the time the color develops. There are other compounds, too, like tannins, that give grapes and wines their individual flavors and aromas. These also develop mostly in the final stage of ripening. The last weeks and days before the harvest are crucial."

"It's all so very interesting," exclaimed Eva as her eyes took in the familiar, yet ever-changing scene before her.

"I've tried to explain it as simply as possible."

"And you've done it very well. But there's a lot to learn, isn't there?"

"About grapes?" he asked. "Or about life?"

Adam and Eva were silent for a long moment.

"Yeah. What you've been telling us isn't just about the grapes is it?" she said finally.

A slow half-smile formed on Juan's face. "The things I say aren't so important. I'm simply telling you what Adam's father would say if he were still here. The only difference is that I'm sure he would do a much better job of explaining. But for now, you must continue to listen to what the vines are saying. They still have many more things to teach you."

It was true.

A walk the following morning through the vine rows seemed possessed with purpose. Adam just hadn't figured out what it was yet. His thoughts drifted back to their winter arrival and how the deceivingly dead appearance of the vines had intermingled with his father's death to dominate his mood. But there was something else too.

Over the past few days, he'd found himself thinking a lot about Doug, his closest friend from college days. Doug had died unexpectedly just two years earlier at the much-too-young age of forty-seven. No warning. One day he was there and the next ...

Adam let his eyes roam over the geometric pattern of the vineyard. Perhaps it was the perfectly formed rows that caused him to want everything to make perfect sense this morning. His memories of bygone days darted randomly in and out among the vines, appearing and disappearing, uncontrolled and unrestricted in any way. He let them meander wherever they wanted. To an era of college fun. To the familiar sound of Doug's laughter. To the fun times and the serious moments the two of them had shared. Before long, the scene before him became blurred with tears.

Two rows away, Eva's voice roused him from his reverie. "Hey! I hope you're listening to the vines over there. You're sure not listening to me!"

"Sorry." Adam brushed at his face with the back of his gloved hand, hoping to catch both tears and perspiration in a casual wipe. "Just lost in thought, I guess."

"Anything you want to talk about?"

He hesitated. "I'm not sure," he answered finally.

Eva glanced across the vines at her husband, sensing that something was troubling him, but wisely resisting the temptation to press further. "That's okay. I'm ready to listen though, in case you need to give me a try."

A while later, Adam rounded the end of a row and approached as Eva busily pruned away excess foliage from one of the vines.

"Okay, I'll give it a shot," he said, taking off his hat and pushing his hair back in place with the same motion. "I've been thinking a lot about Doug recently ... you know, my old roommate from college? It hit me again yesterday when Juan was explaining the vineyard fertilization process."

Eva nodded, but remained silent. Listening.

"He was talking about the flowers that fall away without bearing fruit, without fulfilling their purpose. Remember? He called it shatter." Adam dug into the dirt with the toe of his boot. "Well, that's the way I felt when Doug died. Shattered. We weren't together a lot the last few years, but sometimes I miss him so much that ... I just ... " His voice trailed off and he looked away.

"He was a good friend," Eva responded gently, "and you miss him. Maybe your dad's death has brought all this back to you."

"I don't know. I think it's more than that," Adam ventured after a moment. "I almost feel guilty saying it, but it's like I miss Doug even more than I do Dad at times—or at least I think about him more. It's hard ... I mean, Dad had a long and full life. Doug didn't. His was cut short ... shattered! It just doesn't seem fair."

Eva's silence made an appropriate response.

"I can't figure what to make of it really," he went on. "Part of it is selfishness, probably. I needed him in my life. He was the one guy I knew who'd experienced so many of the same things I did. Please don't misunderstand what I'm trying to say, but I can't think of anyone else that fits that bill." He scanned the grayness of the horizon before adding, "I think about Doug not getting as much of life as I'm getting ... and it doesn't seem right."

Eva let the breezes carry his words away before posing a quiet question. "Do you ever think about dying? Not Doug's or your dad's. I mean, your own dying?"

Adam looked at her for a moment before answering.

"Yeah, I guess that's part of it, isn't it? Intellectually anyway, I know I'm going to die someday. Maybe sooner than later." He took her hand as they walked slowly down the row toward the house. "I guess that I wonder if I'll die before getting it all figured out. I mean, shouldn't we be able to figure it out?"

Eva squeezed his hand but said nothing.

"My life's more than half over, and that's assuming I live to be a hundred. And who knows? Maybe I'll be cut off like Doug. I don't think I'm ready for that ... actually, I wish I'd spent more time with Dad at the end. Maybe I could have asked him some of these questions. We could have talked about how he was dealing with facing death. You know...?"

She squeezed his hand again. "Yeah, I know."

They walked the long way back to the house, but no more words were spoken.

For the next few days, Adam and Eva worked with Juan during the morning hours. Most of their afternoons were spent clearing up legal matters regarding the will and talking on the phone with "head hunters" from various companies around the country. Two or three of these seemed especially promising, though Adam had to admit that his heart was no longer in the hunt with the same enthusiasm as it had been originally. Evenings were sometimes spent leisurely thumbing their way through viticulture magazines they had found stacked in a corner of the small library.

"You know what?" asked Adam one day while he and Eva sat on the veranda enjoying the late afternoon sun.

"What?"

He put down a year-old issue of *Wine Industry Journal*. "Grapevines do best when they grow toward each other."

"Okay," Eva responded, waiting to hear what was coming next.

"I mean the vine's trunk is too weak to stand alone, right? It needs support from somewhere. So when it's in a field of vines, the vinekeeper builds a trellis. If it's just growing in the wild, it climbs a tree or a post or whatever. But it attaches itself to something in order to achieve balance. Then after it's secured, the branches can grow away from the trunk and do their thing. But even then, they grow toward other branches. See?" Adam waved his hand in the direction of the field.

"So what are you saying?"

"Listen to the vines. They're talking again, reminding us to look at the importance of being 'connected.' To be healthy we need healthy connections—you know, relationships—right?"

"Ours is pretty healthy, don't you think?" Eva asked mischievously, an impish look on her face as she nudged his elbow off the arm of his chair.

"Be serious."

"Okay, so what's new about that, Adam? Everyone knows relationships are important."

"But how often do we stop to examine them? What are our relationships doing for us and to us? And to others, for that matter? When I walked out the door of The Company for the last time, I didn't only lose my paycheck. It felt like I was being torn away from all my friends at the same time."

"But they're still there," countered Eva.

"Yeah, only a guy's friendships are usually built around doing things. We work together. Play together. Compete with each other. We don't always have to win. It's just the fun of it all. Maybe after we're done playing, or in the middle of a workday, we'll sit down for a drink or a sandwich and talk. Maybe not. But it's the 'doing' that brings us together. Well, after leaving The Company, my 'doing buddies' weren't there for me anymore. I guess I've leaned a lot on you to fill that need these past few months. More so than usual."

"I haven't minded," Eva responded, her voice soft as her hand reached over for his. "In fact, it's been nice. I've enjoyed it."

"Really?"

"Really. Two of the worst things in our lives—your dad dying and your job loss—they've brought us together in a way we've not known for a long time. In fact, I don't think it's ever been like this for us."

A sudden wave of emotion caught Adam unexpectedly. For a moment he was unable to trust himself to say anything. When he looked at her again, his face said it all. She smiled and leaned over to kiss him on the cheek.

"You did hear from Joe the other day," she said. "You've not been forgotten by everyone."

"Yeah, it meant a lot to get his letter. In the last couple of months, he's the only one of the guys who's written. I was surprised actually, that he would be the one. We've never really been that close. Not much in common. I feel badly for him, though."

"Because he's become a victim in the downsizing cut?"

"Yeah. Cold corporate ruthlessness. It just slams you in the gut, doesn't it? I mean, Joe's older than I am by six or seven years. And he doesn't have a lot of people skills. It's going to be tough for him to find another job. Especially with any kind of comparable salary."

"Have you written to him?"

"No, not yet. What am I going to say? 'Hi Joe, welcome to the wonderful world of the wish-we-were-employed?'"

Eva chuckled, then quickly grew serious again. "How about saying 'Hi, Joe. I'm sorry you're out. Having only recently gone through the same disappointment, I know a little about how you feel. This seems to be a testing time for all of us. You're in our thoughts and we'll keep an eye out in case we hear of something that may interest you. One of the things we're discovering is that endings like this always carry in them the seeds of new beginnings."

Adam turned in his chair until he could look into Eva's eyes.

"Who made you so beautiful and so wise at the same time?"

"I guess it depends on how far back along the vine you want to go for the answer. I hear that 'Eve' woman was a real looker."

Adam grinned. "Yeah, but she was a pushover for the first snake in the grass that came along."

"So?" Eva smiled playfully as she got up and headed for the door. "What else is new?"

Adam jumped up and started after her. Her laughter filled his senses as she slipped nimbly through the doorway and ran toward the staircase.

"Okay, you're right as usual," he called out, sprinting

after her. "I'll stop procrastinating and write to Joe tonight!"

Halfway up the stairs, he caught her around the waist and they fell in each other's arms on the well-worn hardwood steps, their lips shaping a lingering kiss.

"Make that tomorrow," Adam promised as they stood and continued up the stairs. "I'll write to Joe tomorrow."

# *Véraison*

1. During the past decade, whose death has affected you the most?

   _____

   _____

   List the ways in which you've been impacted by this event: _____

   _____

2. What thoughts and feelings do you have about your own death someday? _____

   _____

   _____

3. **Independence** = the inclination to live life entirely on one's own strengths and abilities, without assistance from or relying upon others.

   **Dependence** = the inclination to live life in cooperative reliance on others, taking support as needed from others.

   With these two concepts acting as the anchor poles, the line on the next page represents a Dependent/ Independent Continuum. Looking back over your adult years, place yourself at the point on the Continuum that best coincides with where you were on each of your decade birthdays (e.g., age twenty, thirty, forty, etc.).

Place a "20" on the point that corresponds to your assessment of your dependence quotient at your twentieth birthday, a "30" on your thirtieth year, a "40" for forty, etc.

INDEPENDENCE__|__|__|__|__|__|__|__DEPENDENCE

(a) Having completed the Continuum, reflect on what has driven the changes in your placement over the years. _____

_____

_____

(b) Where would you like to see yourself on the Continuum on your next milestone birthday? Why?

_____

_____

_____

_____

 he weeks rolled by. A few weeds could be seen sprouting in the rows now, but Juan cautioned against trying to curb their growth. "There's no need to turn the ground over just for a few weeds. There aren't enough to harm anything of value and too much cultivation will destroy the soil structure. Besides, heavy tractors tend to compact the soil."

One day, however, he reported to Adam that they did need to treat the vines for downy mildew. Though the past two weeks had seen no rain, the late winter and early spring had proven to be wetter than usual this year. Juan felt that two or three sprayings would probably suffice. Other than a couple of nights during which temperatures had dipped to near the danger point, this was the first bad news Juan had conveyed regarding the vines. Adam immediately voiced his concern.

"Don't worry," the vinekeeper reassured his new employer. "This is a fairly common problem. Just be thankful we don't have Phylloxera."

"What's that?" The term was new to Adam.

"It's a pear-shaped root-aphid that attaches itself to the vine's roots and can even infect adjacent vines by crawling overland or from root to root. There are no chemical treatments that can control this pest. If the infection is confirmed, the only thing you can do is tear out the vines and sterilize the soil before replanting with freshly grafted rootstock. That's why it's important to establish a vineyard with a rootstock that possesses a strong resistance to Phylloxera. Many years ago, this tiny little aphid was responsible for destroying the vast majority of Europe's grapevines."

"The more I get into this, the more I realize that growing grapes is a very complex business."

"If it was too easy it wouldn't be worth doing," Juan replied.

"I know one thing," declared Adam.

"What's that?"

"I'm enjoying this immensely, but I don't think I'm cut out to be a vinekeeper."

The two men were silent. Finally Juan spoke.

"Then your father was right to have let you go."

Adam nodded and smiled as he kicked at the dirt with the toe of his boot, a habit he'd picked up from the man who stood across from him.

"When I was young, I thought this was all my father knew how to do. I didn't realize then that this was all he wanted to do. And now I wish I could tell him how much I've fallen in love with his vineyard and this place. How much I've come to respect the vines. I never knew ... " His voice trailed off.

"Like I've said before, Adam, your father was a wise man. He let you go to allow you to become your best self. He didn't want you to come back to work the vineyard just to please him. You've always been your own person and, whatever that means in your future, you must continue to strive toward that end. He didn't expect you to stay here forever—only long enough to listen to the vines with your eyes and see their life message with your heart. He knew that if you did, you would never be the same. He knew that you would find true happiness and fulfillment in your life."

"But summer is here, Juan, and I still don't know what I want to do 'when I grow up,' if you know what I mean. This has been an amazing respite, but it can't go on indefinitely. I need to find some answers. Make some decisions."

"You're closer to the answers than you think," Juan cautioned reassuringly. "Don't be too hasty."

"Hasty? You've got to be kidding. I've been here for nearly eight months!"

"I know. But don't let impatience rob you now that you've come this far. And don't bother frantically searching for the answers. Just wait for them, Adam. You've made yourself available. Now, let them come to you."

That evening, Adam and Eva went for a stroll down the lane leading to the main road, enjoying the scenes and smells of the countryside as they walked. A dog barked as they passed by the neighbor's place. Eva pointed out a flock of starlings that swooped over the vineyard to the north of the house.

"Those birds are another problem," stated Adam as he watched them zigzag their way into the sunset. "Juan says they're especially so from véraison onward. They peck at the berries and leave them to rot. Then insects are attracted and the juice gets sucked out by wasps and flies."

"So how do we defend the grapes?"

"Apparently that's not an easy thing. There are some chemicals. A few of the vinegrowers actually shoot at the birds. Juan says it also helps to eliminate their nests if you can find them."

Eva studied the seriousness on Adam's face. "What's

really on your mind, sweetheart? It's not just the birds. You've been pensive all day."

They walked along a bit farther before he answered.

"I think it was Joe's telephone call yesterday. You remember I sent him that letter?"

Eva nodded.

"Well, when I talked with him on the phone, he sounded really bitter. Not that I blame him. He's worked more years with The Company than I did and wasn't that far from retirement. Just a few years. I was feeling pretty much the same way when we came up here to say good-bye to Dad." Adam slowed his steps and thrust both hands deep into his pockets. "But I've been fortunate. I didn't stay that way."

"What did you say to him?"

"We talked for a long time. Actually, he did most of the talking. I listened a lot. Asked him a few questions. Tried to draw him out. I even invited him and Ellen up for a weekend."

"What was his response?"

"That he'd think about it. But from the way he sounded, I don't expect them to come. His anger—it's like those birds and wasps. It's sucking the life out of an otherwise nice guy. I can feel him shutting down, but there's nothing I can do."

"Maybe you can pray for him."

"Say what?"

"Pray for Joe."

"You mean just dial heaven and say 'Hello, God, it's Adam. Remember me? I want to talk to You about my friend, Joe'?"

"Well, yeah, sort of."

"You're serious, aren't you?"

"Yep."

"I wouldn't know where to begin."

"You just did—I think prayer is like a conversation."

"Easy for you to say. You're a woman."

"What's that supposed to mean?"

"It's just that women are more sensitive. More inclined toward spiritual things than men. And they can verbalize their feelings more easily."

"Get out of here! What sort of sexist remark is that? Are you some kind of spiritual chauvinist? Do you take every myth and legend you hear at face value? I don't believe gender has anything at all to do with matters of the spirit."

"Really? I've always thought that women were better at that sort of thing than guys."

"Women tend to approach things a little differently than men, that's all. But the quality of one's spiritual life isn't determined by whether we're male or female. I'm not sure about a lot of things, but trust me on that one."

"Okay, but this is important. We're talking about a guy's whole life here—hey, wait! I've got an idea. Juan seems to be pretty spiritual. Let's get him to pray."

"What are you afraid of, Adam? That God might not be there if you come knocking? No, that's not it. Maybe you're afraid that He is there and wants to know why He hasn't heard from you in so long?"

Adam stopped and began moving the toe of his shoe in the dirt, creating a small circle.

"Do you think it really works?" he asked finally. "Prayer, I mean?"

"Of course."

"No kidding?"

"No kidding."

"You don't think it's something that people do to make themselves believe that ... you know ... that someOne is really up there?"

"No, I don't think that way at all. You and I just haven't done it often enough to feel comfortable with the idea. That's not to our credit, I might add."

They turned and began retracing their steps in the direction of the house, now a good half-mile away. Adam took Eva's hand. "Well, if I give it a try—you know—ask God to do something for Joe? I wonder what would happen if I put in for a little help for us while He's at it?"

"I think He's already busy doing it."

"You mean with the vines?"

"Yes."

"But now we need some specific direction. We've got decisions to make about what we're going to do when we leave here."

"Adam, what is it you want to do?"

The tone in her voice alerted him that this was not a question to respond to lightly. He thought for a moment about what he wanted to say.

"All I know for sure is that I'm not excited about going

back to the kind of thing I've been doing up to now," he admitted at last. "I will if I have to, but it's not something I'll be happy doing for long. At least that's the way I feel right now. If I could have the kind of life I really wanted, I'd alter our situation so that we could be together more. Like these last few months. And I'd do something that possesses greater meaning than just making a buck."

"Like what?"

Adam wavered for a second and then took the plunge. "Well, I was driving by the high school campus in town the other day. And I had this crazy idea."

"Tell me." Eva's eyes sparkled with the excitement she felt as Adam's spirit begin to lift.

"What if, instead of getting another corporate job, I taught school for a while? I've got a degree in social studies and an MA in marketing. I'll bet I could get a provisional certificate to teach until I made up whatever course work might be lacking. Several towns within driving distance from here have high schools. What would you think if I took a job teaching at one of them? At least for a year or two anyway."

Eva put her arm around his waist. "I think it would be great—if that's what you want."

"Well, I'm not absolutely sure if it's what I want or not. But in the past, the thing I've enjoyed the most has been developing and presenting seminars and training the new people coming on board. I really got a kick out of serving as a lead trainer in our division during my last two years with The Company."

"If you get a job teaching, would we stay here in your dad's house?"

"Sure. It's ours now. He left it and the vineyard to both of us."

"What would we do with it? The vineyard, I mean."

"That's been on my mind too. What would you say to this?" As Adam began outlining his idea, Eva became visibly delighted. By the time they reached the outer perimeter of the lawn, dusk was settling around them. "I'll get the tea started, Adam, and then I'll be right back. We need to discuss this some more because I've had something in mind for a while that might fit together perfectly with your idea."

And so they sat and talked through the rest of the evening. Ideas passed back and forth between them like treasured gifts. Insights were energized by emotions. Dreams merged with reality. The "bud burst" of Adam and Eva's future, at least in the near-term, flowered into something visible and doable for the first time. Something that met their criteria. It felt right, and promised elements that offered new and exciting opportunities.

The next day they set out to put their agreed-upon thoughts to the test of practicality.

Adam made a half-dozen telephone calls into the surrounding school districts, both large and small. Four indicated there were no openings for the upcoming year. All contracts had been let. One high school anticipated the availability of a full-time position in his general strength area, while another had a part-time opening coming up. Both were interested in receiving his resumé. One principal expressed the desire to meet with him right away. They had several applicants, she said, and were anxious to fill the position within the next couple of weeks. Adam set an appointment for the following Monday afternoon, and another with the second school for Thursday.

On Monday morning, Adam and Eva watched from the veranda until they saw Juan entering the vineyard from the opposite side. Then they hurried out to meet him.

"I wondered if I would see you today," Juan greeted them with a smile, accepting a drink from the small cooler that Eva had brought with her. She smiled back, her eyes glowing with an excitement that did not go unnoticed. He glanced at Adam as he removed his gloves and laid aside his pruning tools. "And what are you two up to this morning?"

Adam, who was carrying three canvas folding stools, proceeded to place them in a small circle.

"We've come to discuss some things," Adam said with a note of seriousness. "Sit down."

Juan adjusted one of the stools and took his place with the others in the vine row, sensing that this would be no ordinary visit.

"Okay. Let's get right to it. Eva and I feel that it's time we began making some decisions about the future—about what we're going to do with our lives from here on out. With that in mind, we've determined what we'd like to do with the vineyard. Because you've been here so many years, we thought it only fair that you should be the first to know."

Juan pursed his lips in anticipation of what he'd known

would have to come eventually. He understood that their decision clearly affected his own future as well as theirs. It was a moment that he had dreaded and now it had finally arrived. He waited.

"During these past months, both Eva and I have come to love this place. Still, I know that spending the rest of my life operating this vineyard is not what I'm supposed to do. It's not my gift."

Juan said nothing, but steeled himself for what was coming. He really had never expected anything other than this anyway. These were, after all, City folk. So they were going to sell out and get on with their lives. And that meant big changes for him and Rosa as well.

"You probably have anticipated that we might put the vineyard up for sale."

Juan nodded slowly.

"Well, for once in your life, Juan, you are dead wrong!"

He stared at Adam, his face unsuccessful at masking his surprise.

"We're not selling. We're staying."

Juan's mouth dropped open, then closed, as a smile gradually spread across his face.

"This is good news, even though I have to admit I'm surprised. I'm glad to hear it though," he said finally, extending his hand to Adam. "Congratulations."

Adam remained unsmiling, making no move to accept Juan's hand or his offer of well-wishing.

"There's a catch to this," he said as Juan hesitated, once again uncertain as to what was coming next. He let his hand drop limply to his lap. "The catch is—if we do stay, we'll need a partner. Neither one of us has the skills and knowledge necessary to be successful in this business. We've decided to offer someone a partnership. Someone whose gifts and skills are centered in producing the finest grapes possible. An honest-to-goodness vinekeeper."

Juan sat without moving. His eyes remained steadily upon the two of them. Waiting.

Adam looked at Eva and nodded.

Eva reached out and took Juan's hand. "What Adam is saying is that we'd like for you to be our new partner, Juan. What about it?"

For a long moment, Juan said nothing. His eyes moistened and he opened his mouth to speak, then closed it again. Finally, he cleared his throat and looked at them both. "You're kind, but I can't accept such a generous offer. This is a very valuable property. I'm sure you can find someone with strong financial backing who would be more than happy to join you in this venture. My son and I have been saving, as I told you, but we're still far from having enough to become your partner."

"You don't understand," Adam responded. "We're not asking for you to invest cash in this land. It's already paid for. Dad left us with a title free and clear of debt. During the last few years we've been able to put some money of our own aside for the future, though not nearly enough to retire on. But we're not interested in simply seeing how soon we can join a country club and play golf every day. We want to do something that will bring meaning and satisfaction to us and others as well. This is our véraison season—our time of 'final flavoring.' Can you see it now, Juan? We're asking you to help us with our dream by helping you with yours.

"In the meantime, I hope to get a teaching job with one of the local high schools. I want to try my hand at working with kids who are starting to think about their futures. I think I can be good at it if the opportunity materializes. I've called around and have two interviews coming up. One this afternoon and another later this week."

"And that's not all," Eva interjected. "If this comes together, then we're going to invest a little money and a lot of energy and turn the house into a bed and breakfast place. This is such a romantic setting. And the house is big enough for as many as four guest couples at a time."

"If I get a job teaching," added Adam, "I know I'll have to work for less than half the salary I was making before. But with the vineyard and a few house guests along the way, we think we can make it just fine. When I'm not busy with school, I can help around here. Eva's an excellent manager and has always handled our finances. She'll oversee the bed and breakfast and the business side of the vineyard. You'll be in charge of field production. It's the kind of thing where we all win. And once we know we're established, maybe we can go in together on a piece of raw land somewhere nearby and develop that into another vineyard."

Juan appeared overwhelmed as Adam now extended his hand. Finding it hard to believe all that he'd just heard, he reached out tentatively at first, then he grasped Adam's hand firmly, shaking it enthusiastically.

"Go home and talk to Rosa," Adam laughed as he soaked up Juan's exhilaration. "Better, yet, bring Rosa over to our house for dinner this evening. We can talk more about it then and, if you both agree, we'll do it."

"I ... I just can't believe ... after all these years ... "

"It's hard for us to believe too," Adam assured Juan. "The fact is, though, I think we're good for each other. You've helped us find new meaning and purpose in our lives at this important juncture. Now we can help you and Rosa. During these last few months we've grown to understand why Dad loved having you here so much. You've become a dear friend. Now we have the chance of being lifelong friends. And partners too."

"I've always dreamed of helping others," added Eva. "By providing a quiet, romantic retreat for couples who need some time to renew their own relationships, I can do that. Hospitality and organization are two things I'm very good at."

"If a teaching job does open up for me," Adam declared enthusiastically, "it will be an opportunity to invest my life experience, both personally and professionally, into some of these young people around here who can use a few more positive role models. I guess I've arrived at that point when just 'making money' no longer holds the thrill it once did. It's still important, but not that important, if you know what I mean."

Juan nodded his understanding.

"I'll talk to Rosa. In fact, if you'll excuse me, I'm going home right now to tell her about your offer. I'm too excited to work any more today." He paused for a moment, as though wanting to say something further, but too embarrassed to proceed. Finally, he continued. "Do you know what means more to me than anything else? It's that you're not offering me a partnership just to make more money. You are honoring Rosa and me with your respect. I'm not so well educated as you and that lack in my life has always bothered me. But you're treating me as an equal. And Rosa too. You can't know how important that gift of friendship is unless you've lived where we live."

Adam and Eva, touched by Juan's words, remained silent.

"Your father was right," declared Juan.

"About what?"

"He used to tell me that you were a good man and that Eva was a fine woman. He was so proud of you and loved you both so very much. He often said that one day he knew you would learn the secret of happiness. To 'listen with your eyes—'"

Adam and Eva joined in—"'and see with your hearts.'" They laughed and slapped each other's shoulders. Then they hugged one another.

For three special people, it was a very happy moment indeed.

# 5.

## Demonstrate your personal worth and value.

"*I thank God for*

*my handicaps*

*for through them,*

*I have found myself,*

*my work,*

*and my God.*"

—Helen Keller, author, lecturer,
college graduate cum laude,
and deprived of sight, hearing, and the
ability to speak before the age of two.

# *Véraison*

*Summer* seasons of the spirit are times of great personal growth. What we've done in the past is now paying off. Still, the responsibility can be heavy as we concern ourselves with preserving what has been planted, with building anew on the life we've invested thus far.

1. How important are the following when you think of your future?

| VERY | MODERATE | NOT VERY | |
|------|----------|----------|---|
| ☐ | ☐ | ☐ | 1. Creativity. |
| ☐ | ☐ | ☐ | 2. Sharing the wisdom of your experience with the young. |
| ☐ | ☐ | ☐ | 3. Enjoying some of the advantages of being deferred to more. |
| ☐ | ☐ | ☐ | 4. Not fighting to arrive anymore. |
| ☐ | ☐ | ☐ | 5. Enriching others and yourself if you can. |
| ☐ | ☐ | ☐ | 6. Putting right value on things. |
| ☐ | ☐ | ☐ | 7. Leaving behind an improved natural environment. |
| ☐ | ☐ | ☐ | 8. Having a role model to emulate at this stage in your life. |
| ☐ | ☐ | ☐ | 9. Staying interested and interesting. |
| ☐ | ☐ | ☐ | 10. Becoming and remaining physically fit. |
| ☐ | ☐ | ☐ | 11. Being a role model others can emulate. |
| ☐ | ☐ | ☐ | 12. Financial independence. |

2. What are you "waiting for" at this point in your life? Are there important personal "life questions" that still need answers? Write them down:

_____

_____

_____

3. On page 131, Juan advises Adam not to "bother frantically searching for the answers. Just wait for them ... let them come to you." Are you a frantic searcher or a quiet wait-er?

_____

_____

_____

   What personal changes do you think might help in your quest for answers?

_____

_____

   List the steps you can take to initiate one or more of these changes:

_____

_____

_____

4. Choose the phrase below that best captures the place of prayer in your life at this moment:
   ☐ Prayer? Are you kidding?
   ☐ I add my "Amen" when someone else prays!

☐ I'm strictly a "Now-I-lay-me-down-to-sleep" pray-er.

☐ I pray in an emergency. Like they say, "There are no atheists in foxholes!" (Besides, if you're desperate enough, it can't hurt—right?)

☐ I pray once in a while, when I think of it. But I usually don't think of it.

☐ I'm trying to make a regular place in my life for prayer, but it's hard to be consistent.

☐ I have a daily time for prayer that I keep consistently.

"Coasting" times
offer opportunities
for inspection,
for finding a
balance in life
when,
having done
your very best,
you
trust in God
for the rest.
This embodies
the Summer
Season.

September came before anyone was truly ready. Véraison had occurred and the final stage of grape growth was well on its way toward harvest.

Adam landed a half-time teaching job that put to use all his strengths and skills. The full-time instructor was retiring after this year. Though the small salary would make the coming year more difficult to manage, Eva and Adam both agreed it was the best way for him to go.

Working part time provided Adam with the unique advantage of establishing himself in the classroom under the tutelage of the outgoing instructor, a man with many years experience. In the long run, he was sure he would be doubly effective with his students for having entered the teaching profession in this manner. He had also been assured that if his work proved satisfactory, the principal would recommend him for the open post the following year. Besides, it would give him time to work with Eva in turning the great old house into an idyllic and Arcadian setting.

Meanwhile, the weather remained warm, hastening the long anticipated day of harvest.

"Just look out there," Adam exclaimed, sipping an iced tea as he leaned against the veranda railing. "Remember how stark and desolate everything seemed last winter?"

"Mmm," Eva nodded, following his gaze across rows of vines that staggered under the weight of their fruitful burden.

"Did Juan say anything to you today about how much longer?" asked Adam.

"Yes. A few days. Maybe next week. The atmospheric conditions have been perfect, but I can tell that he's anxious. Things can change pretty fast in the weather department. He's checking the grapes every day now. Anyway, Rosa says he gets this way every year following véraison."

"So what did you see and hear today while I was gone?"

Eva's brown eyes twinkled as she looked at Adam. She knew what he was asking. For almost a year the vineyard had served them, not only as a place for growing grapes, but as a kind of classroom, a location for reflection and learning. A holy place. A sanctuary whose only roof was the sky. A place to think. To question. To discover.

Here they had begun to assess wants and needs, strengths and weaknesses, successes and failures. One by one, they opened the closets of their souls until nothing had escaped the necessary process of sorting, organizing, keeping, and throwing out. Some searching brought to light disturbing things, stuffed away long ago, taking up much needed space. At other times, their explorations had proven delightful, revealing inner strengths and qualities never fully appreciated until now.

"Well," Eva responded, "did you know that grape seeds are never used for propagating the species?"

He thought for a moment. "Actually, now that you mention it, I don't ever remember Dad planting seeds when I was a kid. He always used cuttings or grafts, but I guess I never thought to ask about it. It was just what he did. And why do I have the feeling you're about to inform me?"

"Well, I'm so bright and intelligent because Juan told me this morning. We were talking about a piece of land that he and Moises have been checking out. He says it's a little less expensive because it's hillside property. But it has possibilities and they think it might be a good buy. It's been in somebody's family for years. They live in The City and have never done anything with it. And now it's up for sale.

"Anyway, I asked him how they went about planting grape seeds in a new vineyard and that's when he told me. The seeds of the grape aren't used at all because they produce a plant that's different from their parents. One that's usually inferior. Only breeders use seeds to encourage new varieties. He says, even then, it requires thousands of seedlings before an improved variety can be selected."

"And so the lesson of the day is?" asked Adam as he walked to his chair and sat down.

"Well, whenever Grandma was around and my friends and I did something we weren't supposed to, there was always a twinkle in her eyes, but she'd pretend to be very stern and shake her finger and say, 'Now you girls better remember, God has no grandchildren. Only children.'"

Adam looked at her thoughtfully. "I still don't get it."

"Okay, how about this? 'God is not impressed with name-droppers and He doesn't take references.' That's compliments of my grandma again. 'He wants you, not your agent.'"

"Grandma?"

"Yep. She was quite a lady. I know I've said it many times, but I wish you could have known her. She was so special—and so full of life! Grandma said she'd always known there were only two choices about aging—either you die young or you grow older. Then she woke up one morning in her middle years and realized that she'd not died young, so she'd better get with the program and make the best of it. Her faith in God was so strong—and she was determined that we girls never forget that God loved us too, not just our parents or grandparents. She insisted that He was always close by and that if we had faith, He would be there for us."

"Do you still believe that?" Adam asked.

"I haven't always. For years I thought it was just Grandma and her simple way of looking at things. But now I'm not so sure. I've been reflecting on what's happened with us recently. Don't you think there's a pattern here? It's as though we've been given this time to get reacquainted with ourselves and with each other. And even with God."

"How so?"

"Well, when you lost your job our financial security was wiped out with the stroke of a pen. I know you suffered, but it was a big deal for me too. Then when your dad died, it felt like life had left us standing out in the rain without an umbrella. Just when we needed to come home and talk about the things that were happening to us there was nobody left to come home to. It felt as though our world had crashed and burned, remember?"

"And then we met Juan," Adam reflected thoughtfully, "and started communing with grapevines."

Eva smiled. "Yes, we met Juan. And the grapevines.

But it's more than that. It's as though all of this, the good and the bad, has come our way to remind us that He really is there. Just like Grandma used to say. It's almost as if He's been trying to reassure us that there is still someOne to come home to. There always has been."

"And this has been His way of getting our attention?"

"Would you have stopped what you were doing long enough to look and listen without all that's happened?"

Adam did not answer that question right away.

Not until the next day, when he joined Juan, who'd been working in the vineyard since early morning.

"Maybe three more days," Juan observed knowingly, spitting another grape seed onto the ground. "Four at the outside." The sun was just clearing the eastern hills as he and Adam met in the middle of the vineyard.

"How can you tell just by eating?" asked Adam.

"Experience," Juan replied with a knowing smile. "It's not something a novice should rely on. There are refractometers and hydrometers that anyone can use to measure sugar and acidity. But there's no better way to measure the readiness of the harvest than for an expert to taste the final flavor. And that's the truth. Here, try some."

Adam popped a grape into his mouth and began to chew. He grinned as he spit out the seed. "It tastes great. Let's harvest today."

"No, not yet. Three days. Four at the most. I think we might begin Monday morning."

"Are you putting me on?"

"No. Determining when to harvest is a skill you develop over time. I'll teach you, if you like."

"Of course 'I like.' I want to know everything about it. But I'll never be as good at this as you."

"It takes time, Adam, like most things worthwhile. I've been at this all my life. And I've been sampling these grapes for the last few weeks. Now that we're close to harvest, what you have to have is a minimum of 200 grapes to test at one time. I took these this morning from bunches growing at different levels on the vines. Some from the top, others out of the middle, and a few from the base. Three berries from each bunch. And I picked from different places in the vineyard, making sure they come from both the shaded and sunny sides of the vines. That way I'm assured of getting a representative sampling. There is one thing though."

"What's that?"

"You'd better like the taste of grapes!"

The men laughed.

**Faith.**

To believe in the reality and truthfulness of someOne especially when based on examination of the evidence.

**Love.**

To hold someOne dear; to cherish and take pleasure in God.

**Completeness.**

To have all the necessary parts; to make whole or perfect.

**Interior Insight #5**

Faith + Love = Completeness.

*A*dam let his eyes wander over what looked to be the most beautiful sight he thought he'd ever seen. As he stopped to take it all in, Juan continued walking along the row.

"Wait," Adam called out after him, "I'd like to ask you something else."

Juan stopped and looked back inquisitively.

"Eva and I were talking about all the changes we've been going through these last few months. Well, I just want you to know how much a part of this you've been."

Juan waited, his hand brushing across the leaves of the nearest vine as if reassuring it of his approval. He sensed there was more on Adam's mind.

"Okay. What I want to say is that Eva thinks we've been pretty lax when it comes to nurturing the spiritual part of our lives ... and I guess I'd have to agree with her on that score. I've been pretty heavy into climbing and conquering—until now, that is. Do you realize that it'll soon be a year, Juan, since you challenged me to honor my last promise to Dad? We were standing right here when you said it was the only way I'd ever find the secret to happiness. I guess you know that I thought you were nuts back then."

Juan looked down and smiled as he dug into the soil with his boot.

"But it's actually turned out to be one of the most incredible years of my life," Adam continued. "Eva's too. In the middle of all the personal chaos we brought with us last winter, we've somehow come to a place of new beginnings. Both of us are more excited about what's ahead than we've been since we were newlyweds."

"And now you're wondering about the spiritual connection."

"Exactly. I don't know where to start really, but I'm beginning to believe that all of this stuff has a spiritual aspect to it, and that you know something about that too."

Juan smiled his thanks for the compliment, took a deep breath, and began. "Watching you and Eva learning to 'listen with your eyes and see with your hearts' has been like reliving my own experience all over again. I'd never before done anything like it myself. And if it hadn't been for your dad, I probably wouldn't have then either. He was the one who encouraged me.

"When we first arrived here in the valley, Rosa became very ill. She looks trim and fit, I know, but she's a diabetic. We had no idea of her sickness, but we'd been here only a few days when her system went out of control. I was the most frightened I've ever been. I was afraid she was going to die. We were so new to the area that I didn't know where to go or what to do, so I called your father. He came right away and drove us to the hospital emergency room.

"In those days, we didn't have any insurance, but he took care of all the bills. Everything. He made certain that Rosa got the best doctors. And he wouldn't accept any payment in return. Instead of repaying him, he helped us take out a medical plan, something we'd never been able to afford. He worked with us until we found a company that would accept her condition. It wasn't easy. There's no question that Rosa's alive today, Adam, because of your father."

"I never knew."

"I'm not surprised. Your father was never one to talk about the good that he did. Anyway, you can imagine I was ready to do anything in my power for a man like this. He only asked for one thing."

"And do I know what that 'one thing' was?"

Juan nodded. "'Stay close to the vineyard, Juan. Learn to listen with your eyes and see with your heart.' He told me it was my choice, but when I said, 'yes,' he made me promise not to give up. He said 'once you begin this quest there's no turning back.'"

Adam smiled at the remembrance of his father's deathbed admonition.

"I couldn't figure him out at first. He wasn't your ordinary man. But you didn't have to be around him long to know that he was one of the most put together people you could ever meet. So I started out, feeling ridiculous at first, just like you. And then ... well, you know the rest because your vineyard experience over these past months has been similar in so many ways to my own."

"So when does the spiritual part kick in?"

Juan chuckled. "It kicked in the first day you made the commitment to search for the secret. Your father helped me see that when it was my turn. He said to me one day, 'Juan, you're a spiritual man.' I told him, 'No, that's for holy men and priests, not an ignorant vinekeeper like me.'

"Well, that was one of the few times he became truly angry with me. His eyes were sparking and he said, 'Don't you ever call yourself ignorant again. No one is ignorant! We just know about different things.'

"Then he explained to me what I never really understood before, that there's very little that separates the physical and the spiritual world. The Unseen is here," Juan held out his open hands to emphasize the point, "right alongside of the Seen. And both are equally real. 'When we die,' your dad said, 'is when the separation takes place. Our body is placed in the earth. But our spirit lives on.' Don't you see, Adam? No other living thing can say that. There's something different about us. The human spirit! It's the part of us that God touches."

Adam stood silent, struck by the profundity of this vinekeeper's simple words. *The human spirit. It's the part of us that God touches.* Of course!

"I believe God looks at us just like we do these vines," Juan continued. "The Book tells us that His original meeting place with the first Adam was a garden. I don't think He's forgotten where He planted any of us since then, do you? The lessons of the vines are really about each one of us—about the seasons of the spirit. See? That's what your father wanted you to know."

Adam looked up at the clear blue sky. "A lot of what you're saying I guess I have known for years—intellectually at least. But for the first time, it's starting to really connect. Juan, excuse me for being so personal, but ... do you ever pray... to God, I mean?"

"Sure. I talk to Him all the time. Just like we're doing right now. It does something for me—inside, you know. Praying isn't always just about asking for things when life gets tough. It's like having a conversation with a best friend. A powerful best friend. I can tell Him things. Things that I don't talk about with anybody else. And if a guy like me can have conversations with the Almighty, you certainly should be able to manage one, don't you think?"

"I haven't really tried praying for anything since I was in grade school and asked God to make Susie Prentice notice me," Adam acknowledged apologetically, "until the other day, that is. I said a prayer on behalf of a guy I used to work with. He's going through a really tough time right now. Same thing as me. Downsized out of his job."

"And did anything happen?"

"Happen? You mean as a result of praying? Well, I think I felt a little better about it. That's something, I guess. Some of that 'inside stuff' you were talking about ... but wait a second! As a matter of fact, I called to talk with him again last night and invited him and his wife to come up for a visit. He's still very angry at The Company for letting him go."

"And?"

"I didn't think they'd do it, but they're coming next weekend."

"Was that what you prayed for?"

Adam looked across the many vines, drooping, languid from their most recent production efforts. The only thing keeping them upright was the support of their respective trellises. That, and clinging to each other. Their load had grown too heavy to make it the rest of the way alone.

"Yes," he answered softly, a sense of awe in his voice, "it was."

# 6.

## Fuel
## your
## spiritual
## life.

# *Véraison*

If prayer is a new thing for you, try some of these prayer experiments:

1. Go to your personal "vineyard"—a quiet place where you can be alone. Speak out loud, as you would if someone were with you—understanding that someOne *is* in the room with you.

    (a) Express out loud your honest thoughts regarding this prayer experiment (trepidation, uncomfortableness, enthusiasm, etc.).

    (b) Ask the God of the vineyard[8] to somehow make Himself known to you in the hours or days ahead.

    (c) Then, be on the alert—"listening with your eyes and seeing with your heart." Remain open to ways that God may answer this prayer. It could be through conversations with others; in books you are reading (don't forget the Winter Views encouragement, pp. 53–54, to read the Bible); in quiet inner impulses or thoughts; or in the events taking place in your own personal "vineyard."

---

[8] The Bible. John 15:1-17.

2. If prayer is a familiar practice, focus your attention on the two-way aspect of prayer—the conversation.

    (a) Cap each time you pray with a "listening" session, inviting God to speak into your heart at will.

    (b) Use the seven *Seasons of the Spirit* Principles presented in this book as a personal list to aid you in examining your direction in life.

    (c) Ask for God's help in applying these Principles to your daily experience in practical ways.

    (d) Invite someone (e.g., a spouse, good friend, coworker) to join you in a prayer experiment. Pray for each other in brief, conversational exchanges with God that both partners can hear. Then talk about your experience afterward.

3. For some readers, prayer may still be an uncomfortable topic, for whatever reason. If this is true for you, perhaps the following will help you get a handle on it:

    (a) Accept as a starting point that life itself has meaning and purpose on a grand and universal scale. If this is true, then it's reasonable to believe that meaning and purpose can also be realized at the individual, personal level.

(b) Whether and how you can discover and define your own sense of meaning and purpose—and in fact, the charting of your entire future course—will be significantly influenced by your personal view of the Creator God.

(c) For many living in the late twentieth century, God is simply a concept of one's own making, a term used to define the Undefinable and explain the Unexplainable. For them the *idea* of God is more important than the reality of God. God is someOne or someThing that assumes whatever shape and form we decide to give it. We become the creators. God is the created.

(d) An alternate view of God is this: He is the great someOne of intelligence, power, and personality, and desires to connect meaningfully with His creation. He is, to borrow philosopher/theologian Francis Schaeffer's phrase, "the God who is there and is not silent." This someOne has made us for Himself and He is the ultimate grounding of our lives' purpose.

(e) Asking this God to assist us in better understanding who and what He is, and asking for aid in defining new direction for our lives suddenly makes good sense. Desiring to know the personal God on a personal level also touches (and allows Him to be in touch with) us at the point of one of our basic human needs. But where do we meet God? In a church? a synagogue? a mosque? How can we know that when we pray someOne is really listening?

We find an example in the Old Testament. God is calling Moses to lead the Israelites out of Egypt. A somewhat reluctant Moses verbalizes his doubts by saying, "Suppose I do this and someone asks me, 'Who is this God? What is His name?' What shall I tell them?" This is the answer he was given: "Tell them I AM has sent me to you."[9]

A bit later, when Moses was experiencing a "winter season" of discouragement and skepticism, he listened as I AM spoke reassuringly: "Now you will see [that]...I have heard...I have remembered...I am the Lord...I will bring you out...I will free you...I will redeem you...I will take you as My own...I will be your God...Then you will know."[10]

The idea with which Moses (and we) are left is that of a participative God-man relationship. A family tie with the source of all physical and spiritual life. I AM, therefore, *we are.*

Centuries later, Jesus Christ risked being stoned for blasphemy by applying this same

---

[9] The Bible. Exodus 3:13-14.
[10] The Bible. Exodus 6:1-8.

name to Himself. "I tell you the truth, Before Abraham was born, I AM!"[11]

Both Old and New Testaments are meant to be the personal record of a loving God doing everything humanly (and divinely) possible to link up with us. To have a meaningful and purposeful connection with us. Our human spirit is indeed the part of us that God touches.

(f) So, go ahead. Fuel your spirit! It's the part of us that God touches.

It's the reason the Greatest Story Teller shares with us an illustrative story about a wonderful vineyard. A place where "no branch can bear fruit by itself; it must remain in the vine ... I am the vine; you are the branches. If you remain in Me and I in you, you'll bear much fruit." Listen with your eyes and see with your heart the secrets of the vineyard and you will find contentment and joy. Even your "winter seasons" will be full of meaning and purpose.

Fueling the human spirit is not a sign of senility, but of sensibility. No less than one of history's greatest and most noble leaders, King David of Israel, once said, "I cry out to God Most High, to God, who fulfills His purpose for me. He sends from heaven and saves me ... God sends His love and His faithfulness."[12]

[11] The Bible. John 15:1-17.
[12] The Bible. Psalm 57:2-3.

*"It isn't enough any*

*more*

*to live with self at the*

*sole center*

*of the personal uni-*

*verse.*

*If it ever was."*

—Dr. Joshua Christian in
Colleen McCullough's
*A Creed for the Third Millennium*

*Periods of
discernible harvest
are for the
enrichment
of others—
and oneself
if we can.
These delightful
"gatherings"
personalize
the Autumn
Season.*

*Autumn* seasons of the spirit are moments of outer and inner enrichment. The former, a culmination of having done our best and then gathering in the results of our invested efforts. The latter, the outcome of our human spirit being grafted into the divine Spirit through faith in God and in His promise of life eternal. Autumn seasons are meant to be times of celebration for the human spirit.

hat should we do about the children?" asked Eva as they drove home from a late afternoon dinner in town.

"What do you mean?"

"Well—there's something I haven't told you." She sighed heavily. "Carrie called yesterday."

"Yeah? Is everything okay?"

Eva pursed her lips. "It depends on your point of view, I guess. Whether you're the mom or the daughter."

"What do you mean? What happened?" Adam slowed the car while adjusting his lanky frame behind the wheel.

"Sometimes I just can't figure that girl. The main reason she called was to tell us that she's decided not to come home for the holidays. Can you believe that? And I got the feeling we're not hearing the whole story."

"What makes you say that? I mean, the thought of Carrie not being with us upsets me too, but maybe she's just testing out her independence or something. Carrie is a free spirit, but you've always thought she'd level off eventually. That hasn't changed, has it?"

"I don't know. This time was different. She started off talking about some new girlfriend that she wants to room with next semester."

"Wait a minute. I thought she was going to move in with Bob and Judi's daughter. Wasn't that the plan?"

"That was the plan, but the plan apparently has changed."

"What's her name?"

"You're not going to believe this. Her name is

Seashell. 'Shell' for short."

"Seashell?" Adam repeated incredulously. "Who are her parents, for goodness sake—refugee flower children from the '60s or something?"

"I don't know. Carrie went on about how they like each other and have so much in common and, before long, she lets it drop that she wants to go home with this girl for the holidays." Eva's voice tightened.

"I asked if her friend's folks were okay with that, and she said that Seashell doesn't live with her folks. Apparently she just 'hangs' with friends somewhere in Beach Town—and she wants Carrie to 'hang' with her over semester break." Eva leaned her head back against the seat and closed her eyes. "I don't think I handled it too well from that point."

"So what did you say?"

"I told her we'd need to know more about this Seashell person before we could give approval for that, and ... " her voice faded as she stared out the window at the passing fields.

"What was her response?"

Eva's face darkened. "Like I said, I probably didn't handle it very well. One thing led to another. She accused me of always wanting to choose her friends, saying she was old enough to decide what she would do for a holiday, and of course, used the old standby of 'it's all because we don't trust her.' We weren't exactly yelling, but it was headed that way. I finally just told her good-bye and hung up before I said something I might really regret."

Adam's jaw was set as he glared at the roadway. Eva's eyes grew moist as she started to speak again, this time softly, more slowly.

"Sometimes I feel like it'll never be the way it used to be with Carrie. She and I were really close. We could talk about anything, and I mean, really talk. None of this bickering and ... " The tears spilled over onto her cheeks as her voice trailed off.

Adam let the silence hold them for a moment before he spoke.

"I guess what I have the most trouble with is that she wants to be somewhere else rather than with her family for the holidays."

"And I feel guilty," Eva added, her tone subdued. "I remember how wonderful it was last year for everyone, and I was so looking forward to the same thing again this year. But I'd almost rather she didn't come home if it's going to be anything like what went on between us yesterday."

Adam reached across the car seat for her hand, letting the confession of her feelings pass without comment while attempting to temporarily end the subject by saying, "Don't worry, sweetheart. I'm sure it'll be okay."

Only he wasn't sure. In that moment, neither of them were very sure of anything. Not where their beloved Carrie was concerned. Maybe they'd missed it with her somehow. Maybe they should have been more strict ... or less ... or ...

They drove the last few miles lost in unspoken thoughts.

"I have a feeling it runs deeper than our daughter hiking off for the holidays with a girlfriend with a crazy name," Eva said at last. "This isn't just about Carrie, is it? It's about us. I mean, here we are trying to get our priorities and goals together, but all Seth and Carrie know are the people we were a year ago."

"So, maybe we ought to make a trip to The City and have a heart-to-heart talk. Let's be up-front and tell them exactly what's going on with us. If we're open with them, maybe they'll be willing to be the same."

"They're young adults now, Adam. I think it'll be hard for them to absorb it, if they're even interested. It's still a little overwhelming even to me. What exactly is happening anyway?"

"Well, for starters, we've taken some much needed time out in order to determine where we are at this stage in our lives. Then there's the fact that my mom and dad are no longer here. And yours are determined to stay in Distant City. How many times have we encouraged them to come this way and live with us, and they keep saying no?"

"But they've lived in Distant City their entire lives," Eva responded. "That's where all their friends are. Roots, remember? Their kids are the ones who moved away. I'm concerned about them too. They're getting up in years and Dad's heart is always a concern, but what can we do? We can't force them. Besides, Jim doesn't live all that far from them and he's good about checking up on Mom and Dad when he's in the area."

"I know," Adam said, "maybe that's all we can do for now. But as soon as school is out, I think we should fly back and spend a few days."

"I'd like that."

"Anyway, let's face it. We've inherited more than a house and vineyard. Like it or not, we're rapidly becoming the 'family patriarchs.' The Company that I hoped I'd be with until retirement is no longer there for me either. I've just celebrated my 50th birthday. As things piled in, we've had to step back and take a long look at where we've been, where we are now, and where we want to go in the future."

"There have been lots of changes all at once, haven't there?"

"And more coming, no doubt. I have a feeling these seasons we've been learning about are going to keep on coming around the rest of our lives."

"So back to my original question. What do we do about the children?"

"Well, one thing is for sure, we're finding out that being parents of adult children is not always a picnic. But, listen, we can still close the gap here. How about if we let them in on what's going on with us ... explain to them how we've found the need to establish fresh meaning and purpose for our lives. If we're open about it and include them in some of the behind-the-scenes processes we've been through, hopefully they can feel more of a sense of inclusion and belonging. If we're going to achieve an ongoing 'adult' relationship with our kids it will have to be nurtured, don't you think? And we'll need to be the initiators."

"What do you suppose their response will be?"

"Well, like we've been saying, they're adults, dear,

albeit young ones. They're growing up. But the fact is, we're still growing too, and that may come as a surprise to them. It's hard to think that your parents may not have grown all the way up yet, but they need to understand that about us."

"Do you think they will understand?"

"Let's give them credit where credit is due. Seth's out of college and working at his first job. Carrie's in her second year now. I thought that as soon as the house in The City sells, she'd be sharing an apartment with Bob and Judi's daughter. Maybe that will still happen. Anyway, let's be optimistic. I think they'll understand. At least I think they'll try. When we tell them just how important it's become for us to make a useful contribution with the rest of our lives, it may help them also."

"I suppose discussing how we've come to this point in time will show how much we want to affirm and respect them as well."

"Exactly," agreed Adam, "and we may even wind up getting a little bit of the same in return."

"Do you think either of them will have any interest in being part of our new venture one day?"

"I doubt it. They're both pretty busy with their own lives. I think they'll want to be on their own—at least for a while—to demonstrate their worth and value to themselves in their own right. Dad gave that gift to me when he let me go. But we can offer them the opportunity and the assurance that they're not excluded in any way. After all, who knows what the future holds?"

"Only God," Eva declared as the car came to a stop in front of their house.

"And after all, it's never too late to start over, is it?" Adam chuckled. "Well, almost never."

Eva smiled at Adam. "You know the part of all this that I like the very best?"

"What's that?"

"It seems to me that the more we fuel that part of us that God touches, the more everything else tends to fall into its proper place. Even the bad things."

Adam turned off the ignition and they sat quietly, holding hands while staring through the windshield.

The late afternoon had been cold and cloudy, and now a few stray raindrops splattered on the glass. A short distance away, row after row of frail, grotesque-looking vines huddled together, their naked branches stretched out once again like the wasted arms of vine-martyrs. And once again, winter hovered a short distance away, behind the hills, tempered by autumn's lingering persistence, filling the moment with a haunting sense of déjà vu.

*What was that?*

Adam suddenly leaned forward, tensing, straining to see through the increasing droplets of rain that beaded and then trickled down the glass. *Someone's out there... among the vines.*

"What is it, dear?" Eva sat up and followed his gaze into the field.

Adam blinked.

It can't be. But ...

The scene seemed almost dreamlike—as did the words that he heard.

And that voice.

No. It's impossible!

*The secret of happiness is in the vineyard.*

The figure in the rain paused and bent forward to run a thin callused hand along a leafless branch. At last, he straightened, looked over at the car and smiled. And—yes! There it was. The familiar half-wave ending at the brim of an old floppy hat.

*Tell it to your children. Be certain that Seth and Carrie learn the secret.*

And then he was gone!

Adam blinked again.

Only the vines remained. And the oak tree in the distance that sheltered a gentle slope near the eastern edge of the vineyard.

"I promise," answered the son, half-startled by the sound of his own voice breaking the silence.

"And I as well," whispered the son's wife.

Rain pelted their faces as they ran for the house.

# 7.

## Know that it's not too late — it's (almost) never too late.

DID YOU ENJOY THIS BOOK?
To comment on

### • Seasons of the Spirit •

or to inquire regarding
"Seasons Seminars"
and/or other speaking engagements
with the authors,
write to:
Ward Tanneberg & Stephen Taylor
at
Spiritual Pathways
PO Box 11952
Palm Desert, CA 92255-1952
    E-Mail Addresses:

    tann@cyberg8t.com
    or
    s_a_taylor@msn.com

*Stories of the Spirit*
True stories that inspire
   faith
      courage
         purpose
and meaning in life!

• An anthology is being planned to include real-life short stories, poetry, and inspirational verse illustrating the "Seasons" Principles and insights presented in this book.

• Stories of historical figures, as well as other persons, living or deceased.

• Ordinary and extraordinary stories of the well-known and the unknown. Men and women whose experiences will lift and encourage others in their pursuit of personal and spiritual growth.

If you would like to share such a story (your own or that of someone with whom you are acquainted) please send it to authors Tanneberg and Taylor, at Spiritual Pathways, PO Box 11952, Palm Desert, CA 92255-1952.

Submissions must be typed, double-spaced, one to four pages in length. Please enclose a self-addressed, stamped envelope if you wish the material to be returned. Submission does not guarantee publication. You may be contacted for verification and authenticity of facts, etc.

# • About Ward Tanneberg •

Dr. Ward Tanneberg, is a well-known minister/writer/ storyteller and guest speaker. His books include *September Strike, October's Child,* and *Pursuit.* He is currently working on another new novel.

Dr. Tanneberg received his B.A. from Northwest College, Kirkland, Washington, in Bible and Theology. After further studies at Western Evangelical Seminary, Portland, Oregon, and Seattle Pacific University's School of Religion, Seattle, Washington, he received his Ph.D., from the California Graduate School of Theology, Glendale, California. He and his wife, Dixie, have two children and two grandchildren. The Tannebergs live in California.

He has served two churches in Washington State and California as senior pastor; as an adjunct professor at Asia Pacific Theological Seminary and the California Graduate School of Theology; and as director of public relations at Northwest College. He has worked with the boards of a variety of nonprofit organizations, and was elected to honorary membership in the Delta Epsilon Chi Honor Society of the American Association of Bible Colleges in recognition of outstanding achievement.

Dr. Tanneberg speaks to civic organizations, conferences, nonprofit and business groups, retreats and churches across the country.

# • About Stephen Taylor •

Dr. Stephen Taylor is the Chief Operating Officer of American Biomedical Group, Inc., Oklahoma City. He consults on behalf of hospital clients, leads educational workshops, and oversees the day-to-day management of ABGI's operations.

Dr. Taylor's educational background includes a B.A. in Education from Northeastern Oklahoma State University; an M.A., with High Honors in Speech Communication from Pittsburg State University in Kansas; and a Ph.D., in Interpersonal Communication from the University of Illinois. He and his wife, Brenda, have two children. The Taylors live in Oklahoma.

Before joining the American Biomedical Group, Dr. Taylor enjoyed a career as a public school teacher; as an assistant professor at State University of New York in Albany, and as assistant professor and department chair at Southern California College in Costa Mesa. He has also served as a pastor; the training coordinator at Oklahoma City's Baptist Medical Center; the director of education and training at Oklahoma Healthcare Corporation, Oklahoma City; and as Vice-President of Education at Age Wave, Inc., Emeryville, California, a specialty information company addressing the challenges of an aging America.

A recipient of numerous awards and honors, Dr. Taylor has also published articles in a variety of professional journals and periodicals. Dr. Taylor conducts seminars and speaks extensively around the country to corporate clients, civic organizations, conferences, and churches.

**If you liked this book from**
**Lion Publishing,**
**check out this great title . . .**

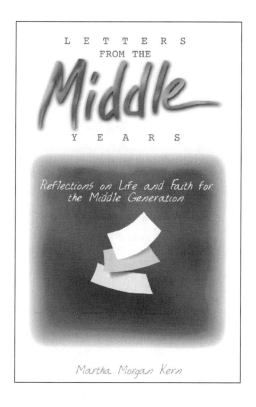

In this collection of 25 soul-searching, transparent letters, Martha Morgan Kern explores the many emotions of life's relationships. She includes letters to her husband, to her young sons, to her mother and father, to her former friend, to pastor, even to God Himself. These letters are personal glimpses into her own life, but touch on universal themes such as love, acceptance and forgiveness.

*Letters from the Middle Years*
by Martha Morgan Kern
ISBN: 0-74593-850-7
Retail: $10.99